W9-DEE-003

ISRAEL EPHʿAL AND JOSEPH NAVEH

ARAMAIC OSTRACA OF THE FOURTH CENTURY BC FROM IDUMAEA

ISRAEL EPHʿAL AND JOSEPH NAVEH

ARAMAIC OSTRACA OF THE FOURTH CENTURY BC FROM IDUMAEA

THE MAGNES PRESS, THE HEBREW UNIVERSITY, JERUSALEM
ISRAEL EXPLORATION SOCIETY

This book was supported by

The Hebrew University Internal Fund

The Louis and Minna Epstein Fund of
The American Academy for Jewish Research

Printed in Israel

ISBN 965–223–958–5

Typesetting: Daatz, Jerusalem

CONTENTS

PREFACE

The Persian period, and especially the latter part of it, is poor in literary sources and therefore known as a 'dark age' of the Palestinian historiography. Written in the last thirty years of the Persian period and the very beginning of the Hellenistic period, the Aramaic ostraca published here shed some light on the demographic fabric and economic reality of an agricultural society in southern Palestine of that era, the range of the dated documents being from 361 to 311 BC. The ostraca presented in this book are part of a larger assemblage whose exact provenance is unknown to us, but whose contents indicate that they are from Idumaea.

Our work started about five years ago, when Mr. Lenny Wolfe was kind enough to provide us with more than 300 photographs of Aramaic ostraca. Of these, 201 ostraca in a relatively good state of legibility are presented here. Among the inscribed sherds published here, 23 belong to the Bible Lands Museum, Jerusalem; 2 to the Reuben and Edith Hecht Museum, University of Haifa; and 3 are in the Collection of A. Spaer, Jerusalem (see list that follows). We are grateful to them and to Mr. Wolfe for enabling us to study these ostraca and to publish them.

The photographs made available to us (reproduced here 1:1) are but part of a larger finding, at least double the number we had to hand. Many ostraca of the same provenance are in the possession of private collectors. About 200 additional ones belonging to the Israel Museum were, for some odd reason, entrusted for publication to a non-Israeli scholar.

We are grateful to Dr. Ada Yardeni for drawing the signature signs that occur in some of the ostraca.

The late Professor Benjamin Mazar was aware of the importance of these ostraca for the study of the history of Palestine; from its early stages he demonstrated his interest in our work and frequently encouraged us to continue with it. We dedicate this book to his blessed memory.

I. Ephʿal and J. Naveh

Jerusalem, August 1996

Number in the present edition	Bible Lands Museum catalogue number	Number in the present edition	Bible Lands Museum catalogue number
13	3168	148	686
48	693	149	661
66	700	150	690
85	663	151	678
86	688	152	680
89	671	153	668
141	677	169	667
143	676	173	672
144	660	182	654
145	699	195	653
146	655	199	679
147	657		

Number in the present edition	Reuben and Edith Hecht Museum, University of Haifa, catalogue number
97	H-2579
201	H-2580

Ostraca Nos. 167, 168 and 185 belong to the A. Spaer Collection.

INTRODUCTION

#1. In the late 1960s and the 1970s the number of fifth- to fourth-century BC Aramaic ostraca from Palestine grew considerably. About one hundred late-fifth-century ostraca were found at Tel Arad.[1] The Arad ostraca are mainly short messages concerning specific amounts of barley supplied to horsemen and ass-drivers and their animals. The horsemen and ass-drivers presumably were related to the Persian postal system described by Herodotus (VII.98), as Arad was a station in this system (Naveh 1981). At Tel Beer-sheba 67 fourth-century BC Aramaic ostraca were unearthed; the texts of some of these sherds include exact dates — in which the years are counted from the accession of a certain king, whose name is not stated — and specific amounts of wheat and barley (Naveh 1973, 1979). Some Aramaic ostraca written in the late Persian and early Hellenistic periods were also found at Tell Jemmeh; four are dockets similar to those from Beer-sheba dealing with wheat and barley, whereas two others were labels specifying wine (Naveh 1992a). Single Aramaic ostraca from the same time were also found at Tell el-Farʿah (south) and Tel ʿIra in the Negev as well as in the regions of Yatta and Raphia (Naveh 1985). All these texts shed light on the history of southern Palestine. The personal names occurring in these dockets portray the ethnic identity of the population. Whereas people of various origins passed through the Arad road-station, the great majority of the people named in the other ostraca were 'Edomite Arabs' (Naveh 1979:194–95).[2]

The state of preservation of these ostraca is not always satisfactory. For example, of the 67 sherds from Beer-sheba only 45 (Nos. 1–17 and 27–54) were legible; the same number was deciphered of the ca. one hundred Arad ostraca.

#2. In recent years hundreds of similar Aramaic ostraca have appeared on the antiquities market. Mr. Lenny Wolfe was kind enough to provide us with photographs of more than 300 inscribed sherds, of which this book includes 201 more or less legible ones. Regrettably, their provenance is unknown to us. However, according to the information gathered from the texts, it can be said that the vast majority were dug out at a site that covers the remains of an ancient town which might have played an important role in Idumaea in the fourth century BC, both in the late Persian and in the very early Hellenistic periods.

1 This date (*pace* Naveh 1981:153) is based on a comparison of scripts of the Arad, Beer-sheba and our ostraca.

2 Aramaic ostraca were found not only in Idumaea and Judaea but also in other regions of Palestine: in Ashdod and in Nebi Yunis near Ashdod, in Elat, in Samaria, in Tel Yoqneʿam, etc.

#3. Of the 201 ostraca listed here, Nos. 200 and 201 should be separated from the rest. Their script clearly indicates a fifth-century BC date, while the remaining 199 ostraca are from the fourth century.

#4. Ostraca Nos. 1–36, the photographs of which were received together, form a specific group within the 199 texts. In most of these 36 ostraca, Ḥalfat is described as the person who provides the goods and the name Baʿalʿid is preceded by a *lamed* — i.e., Baʿalʿid is the person who receives the goods. It can be said that ostraca Nos. 1–36 belong to the archive of Ḥalfat, perhaps with the exception of Nos. 20, 22, 23 (in which the payer is Zabdi). The texts in Ḥalfat's archive were written in a relatively short period of time, within the years 360–355 BC. The earliest dated document belongs to year 45 of Artaxerxes II, and the latest to year 4 of Artaxerxes III (see pp. 16–17, note 5).

Since the names Ḥalfat and Baʿalʿid and the signatures in some of the 36 ostraca recur in some other ostraca (such as Nos. 37–39, 57), it is quite clear that the origin of ostraca Nos. 1–36 does not differ from that of the other sherds. All the texts were presumably found at the same site.

#5. On a number of ostraca a personal name appears at the end of the text; most often it is Zebadel or Shaʿadel, and/or a sign that can roughly be described as two vertical strokes, sometimes forming a V, standing on a curved horizontal. This sign is well known from the Aramaic ostraca of Arad (Naveh 1981:175), where ידוע ב X (Yadduaʿ on the Xth [of the month] + sign) recurs quite frequently.

In our ostraca the signature זבדאל (Zebadel) appears in Nos. 7, 10, 71, 109 and 160 (there is no sign attached to the signature of Zebadel). It is quite clear that these five sherds were inscribed by the person who undersigned the text (in No. 7 the signature is very cursive). שעדאל (Shaʿadel) wrote and undersigned ostraca Nos. 2, 6, 28 and 54 (only in Nos. 2 and 54 is the sign added); יתוע (Yatuaʿ) signed sherds Nos. 65 and 96 (sign in No. 65) and קוסיתע (Qausyetaʿ) Nos. 15 and 29 (no clear sign). Six ostraca end with the same illegible signature plus the sign: Nos. 1, 3, 5, 52, 104 and 145. Single signatures are in No. 33 (זידו [Zaydu]), No. 57 (עבדמלך [ʿAbdmelek]) and No. 100, which ends with נתינא כתב (Netina wrote [it]) and a different sign: four half circles on a horizontal stroke.

What is the meaning and origin of the sign recurring both in our texts and in the Aramaic ostraca from Arad? Although there is no unequivocal answer, the clue may perhaps be found in ostraca Nos. 45 and 72 (there are no signatures), where the sign has the shape of an *alef*. In No. 72 the *alef* is the lapidary form of the letter. Such lapidary *alef*s recur between the various proverbs of Aḥiqar (Elephantine, 5th century BC), presumably indicating אחרן (another [matter]; see Yardeni 1990:132–34). The designations אחר in Hebrew and חורן in Aramaic separate one recipe from the other in the medieval magic books from the Cairo Geniza; see Naveh and Shaked 1985:226–27, 230–35.

#6. The economic reality reflected in the ostraca relates mainly to the cultivation of fields and orchards. Most of the documents deal with raw wheat and barley, or with their products: flour, fine flour, crushed barley/wheat, barley groats and straw. Among fruit trees, vines and olives are mentioned. The word גפן does not occur in our ostraca, but we have the words חמר (wine) and כרם (vineyard). Besides זיתיא (olives), one finds also the word משח (oil). To indicate the types of fields and orchards, the following terms are used: גנת פל׳ (PN's orchard), זיתי פל׳ (PN's olive grove), חלק (field), חלץ (= ?), טור (field), כפה/כפי (garden?), נצב (orchard), and קשת (grove). Terms related to wood are שרי (beam) and עקן; cf. also מובל (load) in # 14.

#7. No. 46 deals with livestock (חיון): one ram (דכר), two lambs (אמרן), one ewe (רחל); No. 118 mentions תורתא (a cow?).

#8. Nos. 16, 122, 140–141 and 180 are related to money, listed in small quantities. Four ostraca refer to 1–4 פעלן (labourers).

#9. The majority of the new ostraca are dockets of the kind known already from the Beer-sheba ostraca (Beer-sheba Nos. 1–12 and 27–32; Naveh 1973, 1979); Tell Jemmeh (Tell Jemmeh Nos. 1–4; Naveh 1992a) and the Yatta region (Naveh 1985:117–18). Many of them bear exact dates (day, month and regnal year) and personal names, which are followed by the merchandise (mainly barley or wheat) as well as the measure and quantity. The type of grain, its measures and amounts are generally written in abbreviated form: ש stands for שערן (barley), ח = חנטן (wheat), כ = כר (*kor*), ס = סאה (*seah*), ק = קב (*qab*), פ = פלג (half), ר = רבע (quarter). For example, No. 9: ש כ 1 ס 26 ק 5 = 'barley: 1 *kor*, 26 *seah* (and) 5 *qab*'. However, sometimes the writer did not abbreviate these words and wrote, for example, שערן סאן עשר ותמ[נ]ה קב חד = 'barley: eighteen *seah* and one *qab*' (No. 63).

#10. The barley is sometimes specified. In the Aramaic ostraca from Arad, barley was distributed for horses and asses, whereas the horsemen received דקיר (crushed [barley/wheat]). In Syriac, the verb דקר in *peʿal* has three meanings: 'to stab', 'to gore' and 'to beat' (in an extended meaning 'to crush'). In Pahlavi, this root as an Aramaic ideogram stands for the Persian word *koftan* (to crush). In Biblical Hebrew, crushed barley/wheat is called רפות or ריפות (see 2 Sam. 17:19 and especially Prov. 27:22). The Peshitta translates רפות of 2 Sam. 17:19 as רושא (barley groats). In our ostracon No. 117 the word רוש occurs. In Nos. 1, 41, 42, 49 and 50, this word was written by the same person with an *alef*: ראש, perhaps under the influence of the Canaanite word for 'head'.

#11. In addition to wheat and barley, these dockets also deal with flour (קמח) and with fine flour: in No. 80, Naʿum delivered, in addition to קמח ק 2 פ ($2^1/2$ *qab* of flour), נשף ק 1 (1 *qab* of fine flour); No. 6 mentions נשיף ס 5 ר 3 ($5^3/4$ *seah* of fine flour). In the Peshitta, in Gen. 18:6 and 2 Kings 7:1, סלת is translated as נשיפא. In Syriac קמחא נשיפא is 'fine flour', and נשיפא דחטא is 'fine wheat meal'.

Wheat and barley were measured by *kor*, *seah* and *qab*. Crushed barley/wheat, barley groats, flour and fine flour, whose production demanded a considerable amount of work, were measured in smaller units: *seah* and *qab*. Oil (משח) and wine (חמר) were measured by *seah* and *qab*, as well as by sub-units of a *qab*: ר(בע) (a quarter) and ת(ומנה) (an eighth).

#12. Straw (תבן) was measured and loaded in rope-bags (פחלץ). This word deserves special attention. An ostracon from the Raphia region has תבן פחלצן 10 (straw: 10 rope-bags). The word פ(ו)חלץ occurs in the Mishna and Talmud meaning 'a bale, made of a net of ropes with wide meshes, containing the freight of camels' (Jastrow 1950:1152b, s.v. פחלין). Since, however, its etymology is not clear, it was often misread and written פ(ו)חלין. Thus we find in Mishna, Kelim XXIV:9; Tosefta, Kelim Bava Meṣiʿa VI:6; Palestinian Talmud, Nedarim 37d and Shevuʿot 34d the following forms: פחלץ שלגמלים or פחלין שלגמלים and פחלץ דגמלין or פחלין דגמלין. Since, however, the ostracon from Raphia region has the plural form פחלצן, there is no doubt that the correct version is פחלץ (Naveh 1985:118). This has now been confirmed by our ostraca; see Nos. 19 (פחלץ 1) and No. 18 (פחלצן 2).

#13a. Besides פחלץ there is another term for measuring straw. In No. 136 we read: נקרו לאלעלי תבן משתלן 7 (Naqru to Elʿali, straw: 7 *mštls*). שתל in Aramaic and Arabic (as in Hebrew) means 'to plant' (משתל in Arabic means 'seed plot', 'nursery'). Its etymology does not justify the translation of משתל as a basket for straw. Nevertheless, because משתל is associated with straw in other ostraca, it is difficult to escape such an assumption.

#13b. Nos. 169–171 read: עפי תבן שדי משתל. The first word (in No. 170 it is עפה) means in Jewish Aramaic 'sprouting', 'branches', 'foliage'. In Syriac עופיא = 'flower', 'grass', 'hay' (Peshitta Ps. 90:5 equals עופיא = חציר), and Syriac עפיא = 'putrefaction', 'stench', 'manure' (Payne-Smith 1903:422a; cf. Arabic غُفَاء، غَفَى = 'bits of straw', 'weeds'; 'refuse of wheat' [Hava 1915:530]). Thus עפי תבן שדי משתל can be translasted: 'refuse (or dung) of cast (thrown away) straw: a *mštl*'. Tosefta Bava Qamma II:7 reads: המוציא את תבנו וקשו לרשות הרבים לזבלים (if one puts his straw and his stubble out on a public road to form dung ...).

#13c. There is still the problem of משתל. Mishna Kelim XXIV:9 reads: שלש משפלות הן: שלזבל ,... שלתבן ... והפחלץ שלגמלים (There are three kinds of refuse-baskets: that for dung ... that for straw ... and a camel's rope-bag). Mishna Sheviʿit III:2 has: עד כמה מזבלין? עד שלש שלש אשפתות לבית סאה שלעשר עשר משפלות (How much dung may they lay down? Three dung-heaps in every *seah*'s space, ten משפלות [refuse-baskets] of dung to every heap). See also Midrash Tehillim to Ps. 2: אינו אומר לו כמה משפלות של תבן מכניס אתה לאוצר, או כמה חבילי קש מכניס אתה לאוצר (He does not ask him, how many basketfuls of straw or how many bundles of straw did you bring into the storehouse?). The word משפלת also has no clear etymology. Is it possible that משתל and משפלת are somehow related to each other?

#14. Loads of wood are mentioned in ostracon No. 25: עקן מובל 1 (one load of wood) and in No. 167: עקן מובלן 3 (3 loads of wood). Sometimes the commodity is not mentioned, but the quantity is given in מובל (load): מובל 1 = '1 load' (No. 129); מובלן 3 = '3 loads' (No. 158).

#15. There are commodities or objects in the ostraca that are not measured, but counted. In seven texts (Nos. 22, 67, 114, 155, 156, 157 and 163) *grgr* X occurs. Generally, גרגרן means 'grains'; but since in our ostraca it is not followed by a measurement, and obviously the texts do not deal with a few grains, it must have another meaning. Ostracon No. 155 reads: גרגרן 2 משתל 1 (2 *grgr* and 1 basket [of straw]); No. 67 registers גרגרן 20 שרי 1 (20 *grgr* and 1 beam). No. 86 deals only with שרי חדה (one beam).

#16. In three ostraca, Nos. 57, 94 and 119, חביה is mentioned. In No. 57 it is חביה חמש (five *ḥbyh*); in Nos. 94 and 119 it is חביה 3. This word does not occur in Aramaic, unless we surmise that it equals חביתא (jar; in Mishnaic Hebrew חבית). In Syriac חביתא is also a liquid measure corresponding to Biblical Hebrew בת in Jos. 5:10 (see Brockelmann 1928:209b). Arabic خَابِيَة = large jar, vat (see Hava 1915:154a). Thus חביה here may be Arabic.

#17. Ostraca Nos. 186, 187 and 190 list amounts of olives that are measured by *kor* and *seah*. The olives are specified by the name of their cultivator — for example, No. 186, זיתי קוסרם (the olives of Qausram); זיתי סמוך (the olives of Samuk).

In No. 187 זיתי מאור (cf. מאור, No. 186) means 'olives from which oil for lighting was extracted'. The word מאור is Hebrew (see, e.g., Exod. 27:20: שמן זית זך כתית למאור [pure olive oil beaten for the light]) and does not occur in Aramaic, except perhaps once.[3] If מאור was indeed a Canaanite/Hebrew word, it was accepted by the inhabitants of Idumaea who wrote the ostraca and might be used as an idiom in their fourth-century BC Aramaic (cf. above # 10, the spelling ראש for 'barley groats').

#18. Ostraca Nos. 188–194 are registrations of fields and orchards. In No. 189, line 1, we find נצב פל' זרע ס 2 (PN's orchard for whose sowing two *seah* of seeds are needed), cf. בית זרע, Arsham Letter VIII:2,4 (Driver 1965:30–31); or שדה זרע, Ezek. 17:5. In Nos. 191, 192 and 194 land is measured by אשל or אשלא (rope); see also the 515 BC Meissner Papyrus (Porten and Yardeni 1989:B1.1), line 3. The exact meaning of כפת is unknown (but see commentary on No. 185). חורא in 189, line 4, could be a personal name, but it can also mean 'white'. שדה הלבן in Mishna Sheviʿit II:1 and Moʿed Qaṭan I:4 is 'a bright, unshaded field of vegetables or grain', as opposed to שדה אילן meaning 'orchard field' (Jastrow 1950:690b). See also in the Bar-Kokhba documents: העפר הלבן (Naḥal Ḥever 44:12, unpublished).

#19. No. 190 lists some fields and their areas: כרם חורי ס 26 (the vineyard of Ḥuri, the area of which needs 26 *seah* of seeds for sowing). כרם recurs in lines 5 and 6. In line 2 the word חלץ appears. This word is known from the Nabataean documents from Naḥal Ḥever. It occurs there in the list of items belonging to the sold field: בתין ודרין וחלץ ותעין; the first two words mean 'houses and courtyards', but the latter two are unclear; חלץ recurs in 192:6. The meaning of כפי in No. 188:4 is also unclear, but it can perhaps be related to כפת in No. 189:4. כפת reappears in 193:2.

Another problematic word is רפיד (Nos. 188:3; 192:4; 194:1). In No. 190, זיתי רפידא occurs. The word רפיד recurs in texts dealing with various sorts of lands. טור, mentioned twice in No. 190, probably means 'field' (Sokoloff 1990:222a).

3 Sokoloff 1990:288a quotes a fragment from the Palestinian Targum of Exod. 13:22 מאור עמודא דעננא, but remarks that מאור is 'prob. corrupt'.

#20. No. 191 mentions משחת (measurement[s] of ...); cf. זנה משחת ביתא (these are the measurements of the house) in the fifth-century Aramaic papyri from Elephantine (Kraeling 1953, Nos. 9:5; 12:6, 15). Here, the word אשל(ן) indicates that real measurements are being listed; one of the areas given is of a marsh (רקק).

#21. The verbs used in our ostraca are היתי (brought), in Nos. 1, 13, 27, 31, 33, 35, 90, 114, 150, 162; and הנעל (brought in), in Nos. 34, 51, 75, 98, 152. There is one occurrence of המטא, in No. 26 (lit. 'caused to reach', i.e. 'delivered').

In Nos. 56, 108 and 128 the word אתגנס occurs. In No. 108 we read אתגנס [פל'] למנקרה. Can this mean 'PN put aside for reserve'? Does the root גנס stand here for גנז (to hide, to save, to store)? אתגנס must be an *etpeᶜel* form, which is a passive pattern; but in the present context it seems to have an active role (cf. התנדב in Late Biblical Hebrew).

יהב is used only once, in No. 16, in the phrase יהב דמי חמרא (he gave the price of the wine). It is noteworthy that in the ancient synagogue inscriptions יהב denotes only a donation of money (Naveh 1978:9-10).

דבר (to lead, to take) occurs in No. 46 in the sentence דבר עבדאדה מן קדם עזיזו ולעדאל חיון (ᶜAbdʾada took animals from ᶜAzizu and Laᶜadel).

#22. ליד קצא (in No. 2) was translated 'to the hand of Qoṣa', but it may mean simply 'to Qoṣa'. However, ליד may also mean 'under the authority of'. On the fifth-century BC Persepolis green chert objects the following formula is frequently inscribed (Bowman 1970; Naveh and Shaked 1973:445–47):

ב X בירתא ליד PN_1 סגנא PN_2 עבד Y זנה
ליד PN_3 גנזברא קדם PN_4 אפגנזברא אשכר שנת Z

In the fortress X, **under the authority of** PN_1 the *segān*, PN_2 made [delivered] this Y [object] **to** PN_3 the treasurer, before [in the presence of] PN_4 the sub-treasurer. Tribute of the year Z.

In this formula ליד means both 'to' and 'under the authority of'. In the first-century BC Parthian ostraca from Nisa ליד is an Aramaic ideogram. In these ostraca ליד פחתא or ליד חשתרף means 'under the authority of the governor/satrap' (see Diakonov and Lifshitz 1960:40)

In our ostraca, besides three occurrences of ליד (Nos. 2, 92 and 98), there are twelve occurrences of על יד. The latter can also be translated 'to' (see Cowley 1923: Nos. 2:3,13; 3:4; 26:21). In a late-fifth-century BC Aramaic letter on papyrus from Egypt (Berlin 23000) we have הבו על יד (line 3) and הבו ליד (line 6), both meaning 'give to' (Porten and Yardeni 1986:48). However, since our ostraca Nos. 34, 37 and 116 have לפל' and then על יד פל', it is obvious that על יד פל' cannot be translated as '(given) to' (the goods could not be delivered to two different persons) and must have another interpretation.

The preposition על יד meaning 'at the guidance, direction of' appears in 2 Chron. 26:11,13; and על־ידי, presumably with the same meaning, in Jer. 5:31, 33:13, and 1 Chron. 25:2,3,6. It is noteworthy that in an ostracon recently published by Beit Arieh (1994:34), the meaning of על-ידי is 'under the authority of, at the guidance of'.

#23. In ostraca Nos. 9, 34, 38, 49, 54, 81, 108, 124, 150 the word מנקרה recurs; and in 15 and 131, מקרה, as a place from which wheat, barley, barley groats, straw and oil are taken out. The word is probably a derivation of נקר (to dig, bore). Thus מנקרה may mean 'cistern', 'cavity' or 'pit' (notice that the words מנקרה and מקרה are not in the determined state). Actually the Beer-sheba ostraca were unearthed in pits, and those of Tell Jemmeh in granaries. The texts of both groups are very similar to ours.

#24. Sometimes the texts specify from where the wheat or barley was taken or brought. In Nos. 72, 48 and 82, we find, respectively: מן עבור זבינתא (from the grain of the purchase), מן עבור זפתא (from the grain of the loan) and מן עבור מסכנתא (from the grain of *msknt*ʾ). No. 92 reads: מן זפתא ח ס 10 למסכנתא ח ס 20 (from the loan 10 *seah* of wheat, to the *msknt*ʾ 20 *seah* of wheat). In No. 81 למסכנת מנקרה can be read. What does מסכנתא mean? Has it any relation to the biblical expression ערי מסכנות, and does it mean 'storage place', 'magazine'? See 2 Chron. 32:28 מסכנות לתבואת דגן ותירוש ויצהר (storehouses for the crops of grain and wine and oil).

#25. Our ostraca do not contain any administrative or professional titles, and indicate nothing about state or regional administration. The socio-economic structure of certain groups mentioned in the ostraca is instructive: three documents refer to 'the House of PN' (PN = Baᶜalrim, Yehokal and ᶜAlibaᶜal), and 30 to 'the Sons of PN' (PN = Baᶜalrim, Guru, Yehokal, Qoṣi, Rammarana, etc.). This feature clearly reflects a clan-tribal organization.

#26. Regrettably, the ostraca do not have clear data about the place from which they originate. No. 100 contains the toponym ערבת חנזרו (in No. 130 the partial toponym ערבת א[...] has survived); the word מלחת in No. 108 might also be a toponym. Perhaps, the meaning of both words, ערבה (desert) and מלחת (saline soil), points to the Judaean Desert and its neighbourhood. The word רמתא in No. 90:2 may also be a toponym, meaning 'the height' (cf. the Aramaic translations to הרמה in Josh. 18:25; Judg. 19:13; Jer. 31:15; etc.). This toponym is very common (in the Hebrew Bible it designates five distinct settlements in various parts of Palestine), and it cannot therefore be of much help in locating the place of provenance of our ostraca.

#27. A clue to the area in general can be obtained from the personal names. Our ostraca contain about 150 personal names (in addition to kings' names occurring in the date formulae). All have a West Semitic derivation. Among the theophoric elements found in about 61 names are the following divine names: Qaus (in 20 cases), El (18), Baal (14), and Yahu (3). The theophoric element in some names is Babylonian/Mesopotamian (e.g., ᶜAbdshamash, Shamashdan and Natansin) or Egyptian (e.g., ᶜAbdosiri and ᶜAbdisi). The verbal or nominal elements accompanying the divine elements are, however, West Semitic, and this indicates that these names are West Semitic. On אדה as a theophoric element see commentary on No. 46. There are 24 (non-theophoric) names with an ו- ending, which is typical of Arabic, including Nabataean, names. One can add to this list 12 names that do not have an ו- ending but contain clear Arabic elements, e.g., אביתע, אלעיד, והבי, זבדאלהי, זידאל, עידאח, שעדאל and שעדי.

The structure of these names differs from that which we know from Judah (from both biblical and epigraphical sources) and Samaria (but caution is needed here in view of the fact that our ostraca derive from a rural population living on agriculture, while the Samaria ostraca originated from an urban population connected to slave trade and provincial administration). The mixture of Edomite and Arabic names is well founded in the fourth-century BC epigraphical material from southern Palestine, especially from Idumaea. From our ostraca it appears, then, that the ethnic structure of the population of Idumaea, with which we are acquainted from the beginning of the Hellenistic period, existed already some generations earlier.[4] Thus, these documents shed light on the economic life and demographic structure of this region during a period about which our information was hitherto quite scant.

For Jewish names see commentary on No. 16.

The vocalization of the personal names in our ostraca is sometimes conjectural. Thus, for example, in the names ידוע, יתוע, קנוי, שלום and תבוי it is not always clear whether they are constructed in the *qātūl* pattern or in the *qattūl* one.

The study of a large collection of documents such as ours reveals features that are indiscernible in a small collection or a single document. Different spellings of the same name — such as קצי, קוצי, קוסי; בערים, בעלרים (and most probably also קסא and קצא); גורו, גור; יוכל and יהוכל; and perhaps also גלפא and גרפא — indicate that the local rural writers did not insist on a standard spelling of personal names and wrote them according to the various ways they were pronounced.

#28. *The Dates of the Ostraca*: Many dockets bear dates. Some ostraca mention only the day and the month but quite a number also specify the year — e.g., No. 62: 'On the 8th of Marheshvan, year 2'. Obviously, the year is counted from the accession of a certain king. In five cases the date formulae also contain kings' names, as follows: Artaxerxes (No. 13), Alexander (Nos. 111, 112) and Philip (Nos. 96, 97; note also אשכר פלפוס [tribute of Philip], which occurs in No. 98 dated 'year 2' without a royal name, which may refer to Philip's reign. See, however, the commentary on No. 98, below).

The years mentioned in the ostraca are 1–19 and 42–46. The lack of documents dated 20–41, as well as the prosopographical sequence of names of people mentioned in the ostraca, indicates that the documents dated 42–46 belong to the reign of one king while those dated 1–19 belong to a king or kings who followed him.[5] The only one among the Persian kings (and,

4 The earliest historical attestation to Idumaea as a distinct territorial and administrative unit (eparchy) is in the year 312 BC (Diodorus Siculus XIX.95.2), i.e., one year before our latest-dated ostracon. Although we do not know whether Idumaea existed as a distinct administrative unit in the Persian period, it becomes clear from the above-mentioned names that the ethnic and cultural nature of the population of the region known from the early Hellenistic period as Idumaea was already determined some generations earlier.

5 Ḥalfat son of Samuk is mentioned in the following documents:
In year 45: No. 1.
In year 46: Nos. 2, 3, 4, 5.

in fact, among all the kings who ruled in Palestine in the 6th–4th centuries BC) whose reign lasted until his 46th regnal year was Artaxerxes II (404–359/8 BC). The ruling periods in Palestine of the kings who followed him before the beginning of the Seleucid era in 311 BC, which brought to an end the reckoning of regnal years in date formulae, are as follows (the length of the rule in Palestine of some of these kings was shorter than their general reign):

Ruler	*Period of Rule*	*Dates of Rule*
Artaxerxes III	until his 21st regnal year	359/8–338/7 BC
Arses	until his 2nd regnal year[6]	338/7–336/5
Darius III	ruled in Palestine until his 4th regnal year[7]	336/5–332
Alexander III (the Great)	ruled in Palestine between his 4th–14th regnal years[8]	332–323
Philip Arrhidaeus	until his 7th regnal year[9]	323–317
Alexander IV	until his 5th regnal year[10]	317–311

In year 1: Nos. 6–8.
In year 2: Nos. 9–12, 28.
In year 4: Nos. 13 (reign of Artaxerxes), 14, 15, 17.

6 Arses' reign ended before the end of his 2nd regnal year; Samaria Papyrus 1, dated 19.3.335, has the date formula '20 Adar year 2 (of Arses), accession year of Darius the king' (see Cross 1985:8*–10*).

7 Darius III's reign in Babylonia lasted until 1.10.331 (i.e., until his 5th regnal year), when the battle of Gaugamela took place. In Palestine and Egypt, however, it ended earlier, in his 4th regnal year, following Alexander's conquest of Tyre and his invasion of Egypt in 332.

8 Alexander the Great ascended the throne in Macedonia in 336 and his reign lasted 14 years. However, his reign over Palestine and Egypt, starting in 332, was shorter. The Babylonian documents reckon his regnal years according to the Macedonian system — i.e., they start with his 7th regnal year (see Oelsner 1974:131f.; 1986:270). If the same practice was customary in Palestine, then the ostraca dated according to Alexander's regnal years — the surviving years in them are 1–5 — should be attributed to his son, Alexander IV.

9 After the death of Alexander the Great the political attachment of Palestine changed several times: Ptolemy I Soter maintained control over it from 319 to 315, when he lost it to Antigonus Monophthalmus. Ptolemy took over once again in 312 (following his victory over Demetrius, son of Antigonus, in the Battle of Gaza) but was forced to withdraw in 311 before the approaching army of Antigonus. These political changes, however, did not affect the year reckoning, since both Philip Arrhidaeus and Alexander IV were recognised as kings, while Antigonus was designated *rab uqu* (=στρατηγός, general) and Ptolemy was considered satrap. (On time reckoning in the period under discussion, see Oelsner:1974:129–51; Skeat:1937, esp. pp. 19, 28–30; Samuel 1962:3–24.)

10 Alexander IV's reign lasted until 306/5, his 11th regnal year. The Seleucid era starts in his 6th regnal year.

The chronology of our dated ostraca ranges, then, from 10 Sivan Artaxerxes II's 42nd year (14.6.363, No. 48) to 20 Shebat of Alexander IV's 5th year (22.2.311, No. 111).

The month name אדר אחרי (Second Adar), which occurs in two ostraca, indicates a leap year. Despite the lack of a royal name in these documents, one can calculate their precise dates: The date in No. 11 is 25th Second Adar, year 2. An intercalary Adar in the 2nd regnal year of the above-mentioned kings occurred in the reigns of Artaxerxes III and of Philip Arrhidaeus (the first option makes the date 14.4.356, the second 17.4.321). A prosopographical examination of our documents in which Ḥalfat son of Samuk occurs makes the second option most unlikely.[11] This examination leads to the conclusion that the date of No. 28 in which Ḥalfat is mentioned — 15th Second Adar, without a year number — may refer to a leap year occurring in year 43 or 45 of Artaxerxes II (i.e., 30.3.361 or 7.4.359, respectively) or in year 2 of Artaxerxes III (i.e., 4.4.356).

Our ostraca contain the names of the months in which 94 or 95 transactions of various goods took place. From these data one can get an idea about the seasons in which various crops (wheat, barley and olives) were gathered and agricultural products (such as crushed wheat, flour and oil) were produced.

	Wheat	Barley	Oil	Barley groats	Crushed wheat	Fine flour	Flour	*p(w)ḥlṣ* Sacks	*mštl* Baskets	*ḥbyh* Jars	*grgr*
Nisan	—	—	—	1	—	—	—	—	—	—	1
Iyyar	1	1	—	1	—	—	—	—	—	—	—
Sivan	3	4	—	1	—	4	4	1	—	—	—
Tammuz	11	3	—	—	1	2	1	—	—	—	—
Ab	6	3	—	—	1	—	—	—	1	1	—
Elul	4	2	1	—	—	2	2	1	—	1	—
Tishri	—	—	—	—	—	—	—	—	—	—	—
Marheshvan	3	3	—	—	—	1	—	—	—	—	1
Kislev	1	2	2	1	—	1	1	—	—	—	—
Tebeth	2	—	—	2	1	—	—	—	—	—	1
Shebat	1	—	1	—	—	1	—	—	—	—	1
Adar	—	1(?)	2	—	—	1	—	—	—	—	—
Total	32	18(19?)	6	6	3	12	8	2	1	2	4

11 See above, note 5.

REFERENCES

Aharoni, Y. 1981. *Arad Inscriptions*, Jerusalem.

Avigad, N. 1957. A New Class of Yehud Stamps, *IEJ* 7:146–53.

——. 1965. Seals of Exiles, *IEJ* 15:222-32.

——. 1989. Another Group of West-Semitic Seals from the Hecht Collection, *Michmanim* 4:7–21 (in Hebrew).

——. Forthcoming. *Corpus of West Semitic Stamp Seals*, Revised and completed by B. Sass. Jerusalem.

Beit-Arieh, I. 1994. An Inscribed Jar from Ḥorvat ʿUza, *Eretz-Israel* 24:34–40 (in Hebrew).

Bowman, R. A. 1970. *Aramaic Ritual Texts from Persepolis,* Chicago.

Brockelmann, K. 1928. *Lexicon Syriacum*, Halle.

Cohen, R. 1983. Excavations at Kadesh-Barnea 1976–1982, *Qadmoniot* 61:2–14 (in Hebrew).

Cowley, A. 1923. *Aramaic Papyri of the Fifth Century B.C.*, Oxford.

Cross, F. M. 1985. Samaria Papyrus 1: An Aramaic Slave Conveyance of 335 B.C.E. Found in the Wâdi ed-Dâliyeh, *Eretz-Israel* 18:8*–17*.

Diakonov, I. M., and Lifshitz, V. A. 1960. *Documenti iz Nisi*, Moscow.

Driver, G. R. 1965 *Aramaic Documents of the Fifth Century B.C.*, Oxford.

Ephʿal, I., and Naveh, J. 1993. The Jar of the Gate, *BASOR* 289:59–65.

Eshel, H., and Misgav, H. 1988. A Fourth Century B.C.E. Document from Ketef Yeriḥo, *IEJ* 38:156–76.

Hava, J. G. 1915. *Arabic-English Dictionary*, Beirut.

Jastrow, M. 1950 (reprint). *A Dictionary of the Targumim, the Talmud Babli and Yerushalmi, and the Midrashic Literature*, New York.

Kaufman, S. A. 1974. *The Akkadian Influence on Aramaic*, Chicago.

Kornfeld, W. 1978. *Onomastica aramaica aus Ägypten*, Vienna.

Kraeling, E. G. 1953. *The Brooklyn Museum Aramaic Papyri*, New Haven, Conn.

Lewis, N. 1989. *The Documents of the Bar Kokhba Period in the Cave of Letters: Greek Papyri*, Jerusalem.

Lidzbarski, M. 1915. *Ephemeris für semitische Epigraphik*, vol 3, Giessen.

Milik, J. T, 1958. Le iscrizioni degli ossuari, in P. B. Bagatti and J. T. Milik, *Gli scavi del Dominus Flevit*, Jerusalem, pp. 70–109.

——. 1961. in P. Benoit, J. T. Milik and R. de Vaux (eds.), *Les grottes de Murabbaʿat* (=*DJD* II), Oxford.

Naveh, J. 1973. The Aramaic Ostraca, in *Beer-sheba*, I (ed. Y. Aharoni), Tel Aviv, pp. 79–82.

——. 1978. *On Stone and Mosaic: The Aramaic and Hebrew Inscriptions from Ancient Synagogues*, Jerusalem (in Hebrew).

———. 1979. The Aramaic Ostraca from Tel Beer-sheba (Seasons 1971–1976), *Tel Aviv* 6:182–98.

———. 1981. The Aramaic Ostraca from Tel Arad, in Y. Aharoni (ed.), *Arad Inscriptions*, Jerusalem, pp. 153–74.

———. 1985. Published and Unpublished Aramaic Ostraca, *ʿAtiqot* 17:114–21.

———. 1992a. Aramaic Ostraca and Jar Inscriptions from Tell Jemmeh, *ʿAtiqot* 21:49–53.

———. 1992b. *On Sherd and Papyrus: Aramaic and Hebrew Inscriptions from the Second Temple, Mishnaic and Talmudic Periods*, Jerusalem (in Hebrew).

Naveh, J., and Shaked, S. 1973. Ritual Texts or Treasury Documents? *Orientalia* 42:445–57.

———. 1985. *Amulets and Magic Bowls: Aramaic Incantations of Late Antiquity*, Jerusalem-Leiden.

Oelsner, J. 1974. Keilschriftliche Beiträge zur politischen Geschichte Babyloniens in den ersten Jahrzehnten der griechischen Herrschaft (331–305 v.u.Z.), *Altorientalische Forschungen* 1:129–151.

———. 1986. *Materialien zur babylonischen Gesellschaft und Kultur in hellenistischer Zeit*, Budapest.

Payne-Smith, R. 1903. *A Compendious Syriac Dictionary*, Oxford.

Porten, B., and Yardeni, A. 1986. *Textbook of Aramaic Documents from Ancient Egypt*, vol. 1: *Letters*, Jerusalem.

———. 1989. *Textbook of Aramaic Documents from Ancient Egypt*, vol. 2: *Contracts*, Jerusalem.

Postgate, J. N. 1974. *Taxation and Conscription in the Assyrian Empire*, Rome.

Samuel, A. E. 1962. *Ptolemaic Chronology*, Munich (=*Münchner Beiträge zur Papyrus-forschung und antiken Rechtsgeschichte* 43).

Skeat, T. C. 1937. The Reigns of the Ptolemies, with tablets for converging Egyptian dates to the Julian system, *Mizraim* 6:7–40.

Sokoloff, M. 1990. *A Dictionary of Jewish Palestinian Aramaic of the Byzantine Period*, Ramat-Gan.

Yadin, Y. 1962. Expedition D — The Cave of the Letters, *IEJ* 12:227–57.

Yadin, Y., and Naveh, J. 1989. The Aramaic and Hebrew Ostraca and Jar Inscriptions, in *Masada*, I, Jerusalem, pp. 1–68.

Yardeni, A. 1990. New Jewish Aramaic Ostraca, *IEJ* 40:130–52.

Zadok, R. 1979. *The Jews in Babylonia during the Chaldean and Achaemenian Periods According to the Babylonian Sources*, Haifa.

ABBREVIATIONS

BASOR	*Bulletin of the American Schools of Oriental Research*
CAD	*The Assyrian Dictionary of the Oriental Institute of the University of Chicago*
DJD	*Discoveries in the Judaean Desert*
IEJ	*Israel Exploration Journal*
KAI	H. Donner and W. Röllig, *Kanaanäische und aramäische Inschriften*, vols. I–III, Wiesbaden 1962–1964

TEXTS, TRANSLATIONS AND COMMENTARY

1	On the 3rd of Iyyar, year 45. Ḥalfat brought to Ba^{c}al^{c}id son of Ḥuri, from the grind of *Mšby* that he gave ... barley groats: 2 *seah*, 3 *qab*. (sign + signature)	ב 3 לאיר שנת 45 היתי חלפת לבעלעיד בר חורי מן טחון משבי זי נתן ... ראש ס 2 ק 3 ...
2	On the 20th of Tammuz, year 46. Ḥalfat to the hand of Qoṣa, which is in (the) pit, wheat: 1 *kor*, 3 *seah*. Sha^{c}adel (sign)	ב 20 לתמוז שנת 46 חלפת ליד קצא זי במנקרה ח̄ כ̄ 1̄ ס̄ 3̄ שע[דא]ל
3	On the 22nd of Sivan, year 46. Ḥalfat to Ba^{c}al^{c}id son of Ḥuri, fine flour: 2 *seah*; flour: 2 *seah*, 1 *qab*. (sign + signature)	ב 22 לסיון שנת 46 חלפת לבעלעיד בר חורי נשיף ס 2 קמח ס 2 ק 1 ...
4	On the 6th of Tammuz, year 46. Ḥalfat to Ba^{c}al^{c}id son of Ḥuri, from the later grind, flour: 3 *seah*, 3 *qab*.	ב 6 לתמוז שנת 46 חלפת לבעלעיד בר חורי מן טחונא אחריא ק̄מ̄ח̄ ס 3 ק 3

On Nos. 1–36 as a specific group see Introduction, #4.

1 5.5.360 BC

טחון means 'grind'. טחון משבי is not clear enough; might משבי be a personal name? See below, commentary on Nos. 4–5.

For ראש and its spelling see Introduction, #10.

On signs and signatures see Introduction, #5.

2 8.8.359 BC

For ליד and עליד see Introduction, #22.

The name קצא presumably equals קוסי, קסא, קוצי, קצי. These names should be disassociated from the Edomite divine name קוס because: (a) The letter *waw* — missing in קסי — is an essential component of קוס; (b) It seems improbable that the name of the Edomite national god קוס was misspelled in Idumaea and became קוץ.

For מנקרה see Introduction, #23.

3 12.7.359 BC

For נשיף see Introduction, #11.

4–5 טחונא אחריא means 'the last grind', 'the later grind'. This can perhaps be compared with the expression הקמח הראשון (the first flour), occurring in a Hebrew ostracon from Arad (Aharoni 1981:12–13).

4 25.7.359 BC

1

2

3

4

5	On the 19th of Tammuz, year 46.	ב 19 לתמוז שנת 46
	Ḥalfat to Ba^cal^cid, from the later	חלפת לבעליד מן טחונא
	grind, fine flour: 1 *seah*, 2 *qab*;	אחריא נשיף ס 1 ק 2
	flour: . . .	קמ̄ח . . .
	(sign + signature)	צ . . .
6	On the 4th of Elul, year 1.	ב 4 לאלול שנת 1
	Ḥalfat, fine flour: 5¾ *seah*;	חלפת נשיף ס 5 ר 3
	flour: 2 *seah*, 2 *qab*.	קמח ס 2 ק 2
	Sha^cadel	שעדאל
7	On the 11th of Elul, year 1 (or 10).	ב 11 לאלול שנת 1 (10?)
	Ḥalfat, fine flour: 5 *qab*;	חלפת נשיף ק 5
	flour: 1 *seah*, 2 *qab*.	קמח ס 1 ק 2
	Zebadel	זבדאל
8	On the 23rd of Elul, year 1.	ב 23 לאלול שנת 1
	Ḥal[fat], wheat: 4 *seah*,	חל̄[פת] ח ס 4
	4 *qab*, 1 *b*.	ק 4 ב 1
9	On the 4th of Sivan, year 2.	ב 4 לסיון [שנ]ת 2
	Ḥalfat, from (the) pit, to Ba^cal^cid,	חלפת מן מנקרה לבעליד̄
	barley: 1 *kor*, 26 *seah*, 5 *qab*.	ש כ 1 ס 26 ק 5
10	On the 24th of Ab, year 2.	ב 24 לאב שנת 2
	Ḥalfat, barley: 6 *seah* (and) half a *qab*.	חלפת ש ס 6 פ̄לג ק̄ב̄
	Zebadel	זבדאל

5 7.8.359 BC

6 10.9.358 BC

7 17.9.358 BC. For prosopographical reasons the reading ‘year 1’ is preferable. For the reading זבדאל see Introduction, #5.

8 29.9.358 BC. For ב 1, see commentary on No. 107.

9 1.6.357 BC

10 19.8.357 BC

5
6
7
8
9
10

11	On the 25th of Second Adar, year 2. Ḥalfat Son of Samuk, oil: 2 *qab*, 2 quarters, 1 eighth.	25 לאדר אחרי נת 2 חלפת בר סמוך שח ק 2 ר 2 ת 1
12	Ḥalfat, wheat: 2 *seah*, 2 *qab*. On the 22nd of Sivan, year 2.	לפת ח ס 2 ק 2 22 לסיון שנת 2
13	On the 16th of Tammuz, year 4 of Artaxerxes the king. Ḥalfat brought barley: 1 *kor*, 12 *seah*, 3 *qab*; wheat: 1 *kor*, 5 *seah*, 4 *qab*.	16 לתמוז שנת 4 רתחשסש מלכא היתי לפת ש כר 1 ס 12̄ ק 3 כ 1 ס 5 ק̄ 4
14	On the 22nd of Tammuz, year 4. Ḥalfat to Ba^cal^ci[d], barley: 15 *seah* . . .	22 לתמוז שנת 4 לפת לבעלעי[ד] ס 15 . . .
15	On the 4th of Shebat, year 4. Ḥalfat, from (the) pit, wheat: 12 *seah* (and) a *qab*. Qaus[yeta^c]	4 לשבט שנת 4 לפת מן̄ מקרה̄ סאן תרי 10 קב וס[יתע]
16	On the 28th of Kislev, Ḥalfat gave Yeho^canah the price of the wine, 8 *ma^cah*.	28 לכסלו הב חלפת ליהוענה מי חמרא מ 8

---

11 14.4.356 BC

The expression '2 quarters of a *qab*' (instead of 'half a *qab*') suggests that the volume of the container used to measure the oil in this case was a quarter of a *qab*, not half a *qab*.

We are grateful to Prof. M. Sokoloff for drawing our attention to ת = תומנה.

12 19.6.357 BC

13 21.7.355 BC

14 27.7.355 BC

15 1.2.354 BC

מקרה presumably equals מנקרה.

ח סאן תרי 10. The mixed way of writing 12, can be compared with [בע]סרין 1 כסלו (on the 21st of Kislev), in a deed from the time of the Bar-Kokhba revolt (see Naveh 1992b:86). Likewise, No. 135 has מא ו 44 (=144).

16 יהוענה, one of the few persons bearing a Yahwistic name in our ostraca, may be a non-resident wine merchant. Also עבדיהו (in No. 148), whose name, preceded by a *lamed*, is written on a sherd, must not be counted with the inhabitants of the community. טביו (in Nos. 174 and 183) may be the Hebrew name Ṭubyau (see below the fifth-century BC name list, No. 201:4), but it may also be an Arabic name ending with -u. The only person with a Yahwistic name who seems to be a part of people reflected in our ostraca is יהוכל. He is the head of a family whose descendants bear non-Yahwistic names.

11

12

13

14

15

16

17	On the 25th of Shebat, year 4. Ḥalfat, oil: 1 eighth (*qab*).	ב 25 לשבט שנת 4 חלפת משח ת 1
18	Ḥalfat to Ba^{c}al^{c}id, 2 sacks (of straw).	חלפת לבעלעיד פחלצן 2
19	Zabdi to Ba^{c}al^{c}id, 1 sack (of straw). On the 10th of Elul.	זבדי לבעלעיד פחלץ 1 ב 10 לאלול
20	Zabdi to Ba^{c}al^{c}id, 1 sack (of straw).	זבדי לבעלעיד פחלץ 1
21	Ḥalfat to Ba^{c}al^{c}id, . . .	חלפת לבעלעיד . . .
22	Zabdi to Ba^{c}al^{c}id, 14 *grgr*. On the 30th of Marheshvan.	זבדי לבעלעיד גרגרן 14 ב 30 למרחשון

---

17 22.2.354 BC

18 For פחלץ see Introduction, #12.

22 For גרגרן see Introduction, #15.

17

18

19

20

21

22

23	Zabdi to Ba^{c}al^{c}id,	זבדי לבעלעיד
	2 sacks (of straw).	פחלצן 2
24	On the 25th, Ḥanael,	ב 25 חנאל
	12 baskets (of straw).	משתלן 12
	Ba^{c}al^{c}id, on the 26th,	בעלעיד ב 26
	8 baskets (of straw).	משתלין 8
25	Ḥalfat to Ba^{c}al^{c}id	חלפת לבעלעיד
	son of Ḥuri, 1 load of wood.	בר חורי עקן מובל 1
26	Ḥalfat delivered	המטא חלפת
	from . . . fine flour:	מן . . . נשיף
	X *seah* . . .	ס . . .
	. . .	. . .
27	Ḥalfat brought	היתי חלפת
	. . .	. . .
28	Ḥalfat, 50	חלפת מסמרן
	pegs (nails). On the 15th of	50 ב 15
	Second Adar.	לאדר אחרי
	Sha^{c}adel	שעדאל

---

24 For משתלן see Introduction, #13. This word occurs in El-Kom Ostracon No. 8, reading: חזאל תבן משתלין 2 (Ḥazael, 2 baskets of straw) (thanks are due to Prof. Lawrence Geraty for the photographs of the late-fourth-century BC El-Kom ostraca). In a third-century BC Aramaic ostracon from Egypt, a letter to Leptines (see Lidzbarski 1915:22–25), Ada Yardeni (who was not aware of the word משתל in our ostraca) read in line 9: וזינא במשתלא חתם (personal communication), which should be translated 'and the weapon is sealed in the (straw) basket'.

28 30.3.361 or 7.4.359 or 4.4.356 BC (see Introduction, #28).
All the other documents point to Ḥalfat as a source of agricultural products (raw wheat and barley and their products in various stages of processing, as well as oil and wood). It seems reasonable to assume, therefore, that the מסמרן in this document are (wooden) pegs rather than metal nails, which are not produced by farmers.

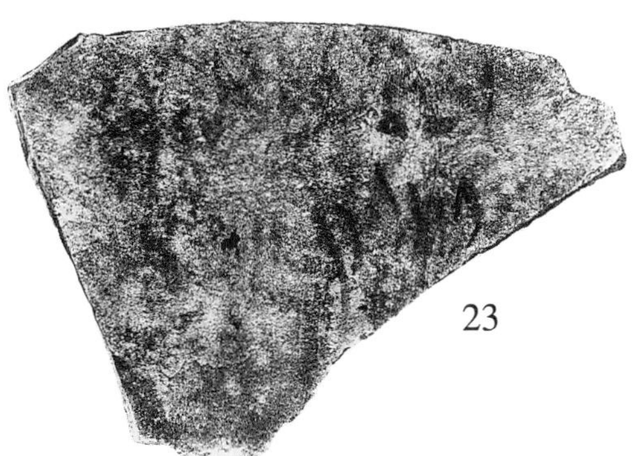
23

24

25

26

27

28

29	Ḥalfat, barley: 3 *kor*, 2 *seah*; wheat: 2 *seah*. Qausyata[c]	חלפת ש̄ כ̄ 3 ס 2 ח ס 2 קוסיתע
30	Ḥalfat, fine flour: 1 1/2 *qab*; flour: 2 *qab*.	חלפת נשיף ק 1 פ קמח ק 2
31	On the 4th of Ab, Ḥalfat brought wheat: 20 [*seah*]; and barley: 29 *seah*, 5 *qab*.	ב 4 לאב היתי חלפת ח [ס] 20 וש ס 29 ק 5
32	Ḥalfat, oil: 1 *seah*, 1 *qab* (and) half a *qab*.	חלפת משח ס 1 ק 1̄ פלג קב
33	Ḥalfat brought, on the 15th of Sivan, barley: 2 *kor*, 4 *seah*. Zaydu	היתי חלפת ב 15 לסיון ש כרן 2 ס 4 זידו
34	Ḥalfat brought in from (the) pit to Abiyeta[c], under the authority of . . ., wheat: 2 *kor*, X *seah*, 3 *qab*; barley: 6 *kor*.	הנעל חלפת מן מנקרה לאביתע על יד . . . ח כרן 2 ס . . . ק 3 שערן כרן 6

---

31 One should notice the precision of the barley measuring in this document: Its quantity is 1 *kor* less 1 *qab* (1:180 of a *kor*). Certainly it was not measured with either a *kor* or a *qab* container (which are too large or too small, respectively). It stands to reason that it was measured with a *seah* (or two-*seahs*) container and eventually, when the last *seah* was not full, they used *qab* measurements.

34 For the translation of על יד, see Introduction, #22.

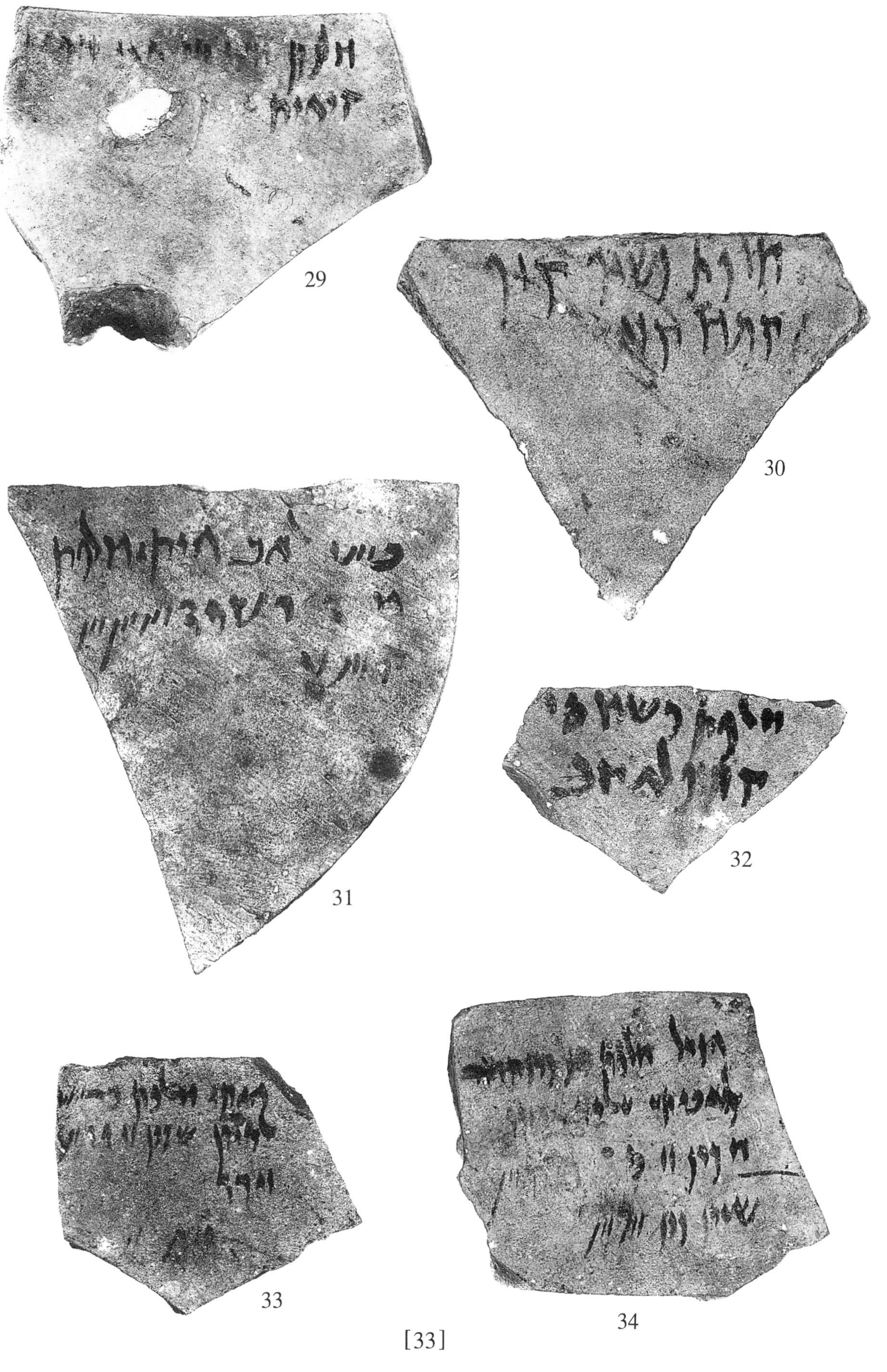

29

30

31

32

33

34

35	On the 3rd of Tammuz, Ḥalfat	ב 3 לתמוז היתי
	brought the wheat.	חלפת חנטיא
	Wheat: 3 *kor*, 2 *seah*, 1 *qab*.	ח כרן 3 ס̄ 2 ק 1
	Zaydu . . .	זידו נב[ ]
36	[^{c}A]ni, baskets (of straw): 10(?)	[ע]ני משתלן 10(?)
	(+)7	7
37	^{c}Abdi to Ba^{c}al^{c}id,	עבדי לבעלעיד
	1½ baskets (of straw) under the authority of	משתל 1 פ על יד
	Amitai. On the 20th of Ab.	אמתי ב 20 לאב
38	Zabdi to Ba^{c}al^{c}id, from	זבדי לבעלעיד מן
	(the) pit, 1 sack (of straw).	מנקרה פ̄וחלץ̄ 1
	On the 13th of Si[van].	ב 13 לס[יון]
39	To the grove . . .	לקשת[. . .]
	. . .	. . . [
	Shamash[. . .	שמש[. . .]
	. . . son of Ba^{c}al^{c}id son of . . .	. . . בר בעלעיד בר [ ]
	. . .	[ ]
40	The grove of S[ ]	קשת ס[ ]
	Netansin son of G[ ]	נתנסין בר ג[ ]

36 The number 17 is written here in two lines.

39 The designation here of the son of Ba^{c}al^{c}id encompassed the names of three generations.

39–40 קשת. This is a loan word, deriving from Akkadian *qištu*, (forest, grove). On other derivates of this word, קיסא and קינסא, in Syriac and other Aramaic dialects, see Kaufman 1974:86.

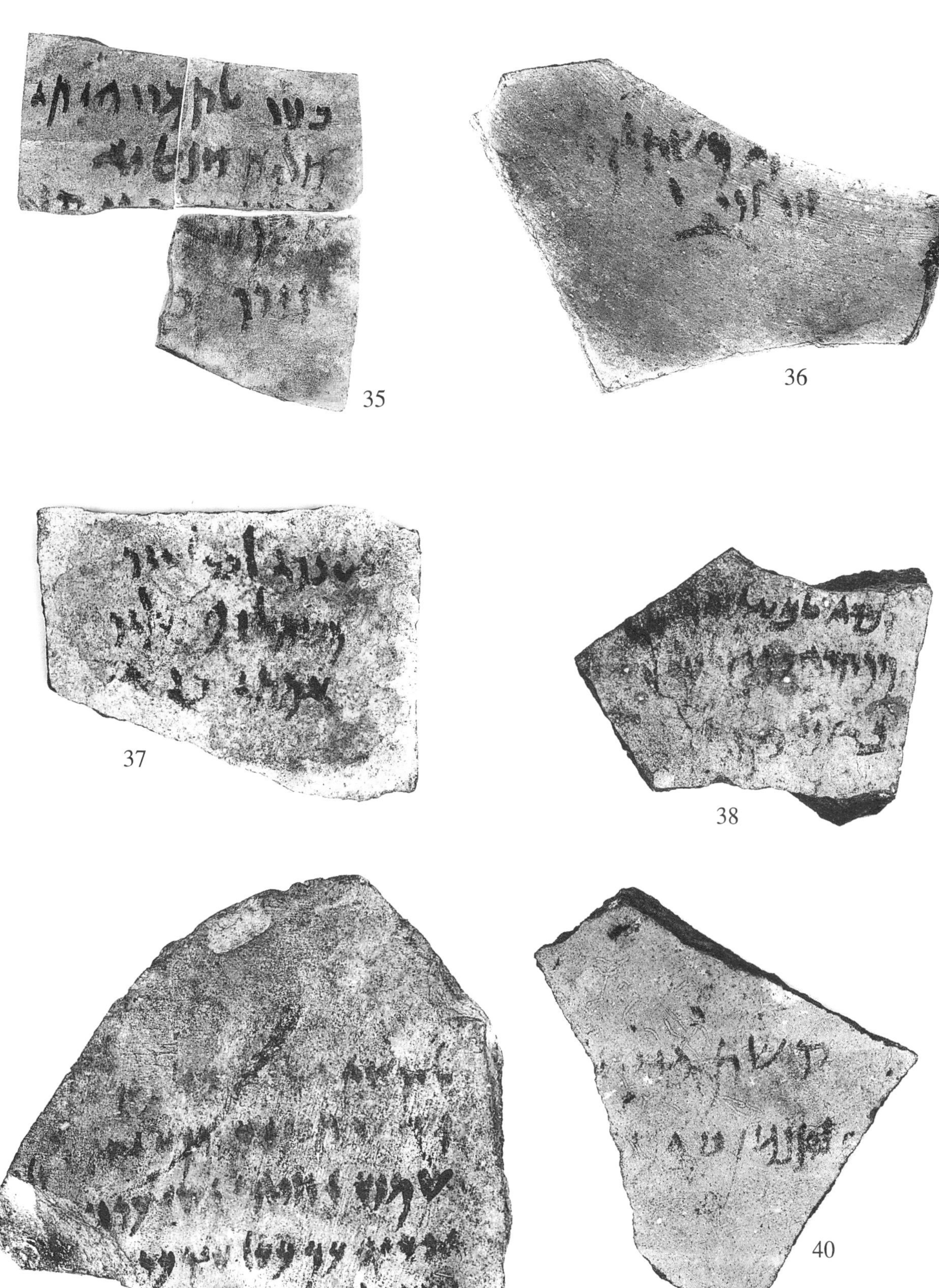

35 36 37 38 39 40

41	Namru to La^{c}ade[l] from the Sons of ^{c}Alba^{c}al, barley groats: 4 *qab*. On the 9th of Kislev, [ye]ar . . .	נמרו ללעדא[ל] מן בני עלבעל ראש ק 4 ב 9 לכסלו [שנ]ת [. . .]
42	[La^{c}a]del from the Sons of ^{c}Alba^{c}al, that of Adar and Nisan, barley groats: 3 *seah*, 3 *qab*. On the 22nd of Sivan.	[לע]דאל מן בני עלבעל זי אדר וניסן ראש ס 3 ק 3 ב 22 לסיון
43	On the 22nd of Sivan, y[ear X]. Zabdi to La^{c}adel . . . Yati^{c}el	ב 22 לסיון ש[נת . . .] זבדי ללעדאל [ ] יתיעאל [ ] . . .
44	La^{c}adel, flour: 2 *seah*; and Qosa, wheat: 10 *seah*. On the 1st of Marheshvan.	לעדאל קמח ס 2 וקסא ח ס 10 ב 1 למרחשון
45	Zabdi to La^{c}adel, 2 baskets (of straw). (sign)	זבדי ללעדאל משתלן 2
46	On the 13th of Tebeth, ^{c}Abd$^{\supset}$ada took/drove from ^{c}Azizu and La^{c}adel 4 animals: 1 ram, 2 lambs, 1 ewe.	ב 13 לטבת דבר עבדאדה מן קדם עזיזו ולעדאל חיון 4 דכר 1 אמרן 2 רחל 1

46 The personal names עבדאדה and זבדאדה indicate that אדה is a theophoric element so far unknown. עבדאדה now can be read in Beer-sheba Ostracon No. 7 (instead of נבואלה; Naveh 1973:80). Is אדה a derivative of הדד? In a late-seventh- or sixth-century BC Aramaic seal (Hecht Museum, Haifa, No. H/1489: see Avigad 1989, No. 20, and Avigad forthcoming, No. 790) the name והבדה is inscribed. The components of this name are presumably the Arabic verb והב and the theophoric element אדה.

41

42

43

44

45

46

47	La^{c}adel son of Q[. . .] wheat: 20 *seah*, from the grain of the loan; the storehouse of ^{c}Adarba^{c}al	לעדאל בר ק[ ] ח ס 20 מן עבור זפתא מסכנת [ע]דרבעל
48	On the 10th of Sivan, year 42. L[. . .] Fine flour: 6 *qab*; wheat: 7 *seah*, 5 *qab*.	ב 10 לסיון שנת 42 ל[. . .] נש[יף] ק 6 ח ס 7 ק 5
49	^{c}Abdba^{c}al to Marṣe^{c}at son of Qoṣi, from (the) pit, barley groats: 5 *seah*. On the 26th of Nisan, year 44.	עבדבעל למרצעת בר קוצי מן מנקרה ראש ס 5 ב 26 לניסן שנת 44
50	On the 30th of Tebeth, year 44. ^{c}Abd$^{\supset}$ada to La^{c}adel, barley groats: 1 *seah*, 1 *qab* (signature and sign)	ב 30 לטבת שנת 44 עבדאדה ללעדאל [ר]אש ס 1 ק 1 . . . צ
51	On the 18th of Ab, year 46. Qanuy brought in . . . barley: 8 *seah*, 3 *qab*.	ב 18 לאב שנת 46 הנעל קנוי [ ] ש ס 8 ק 3
52	On the 22nd of Sivan, year 46. Samku to Qaushanan, fine flour: 2 *seah* 2 *qab*; flour: 2 *seah*, 2 *qab*. (a sign)	ב 22 לסיון שנת 46 סמכו לקוסחנן נשיף ס 2 ק 2 קמח ס 2 ק 2 X

---

47 For עבור זפתא and מסכנתא see Introduction, #24.

48 One should notice that 6 *qab* equal 1 *seah*.

49 10.5.361 BC
The occurrence of the name מרצעת here and in Nos. 159, 172 and 175 enabled us to read this name in an ostracon from Yatta, line 2 (Naveh 1985:117).

50 3.2.360 BC

51 5.9.359 BC

52 12.7.359 BC

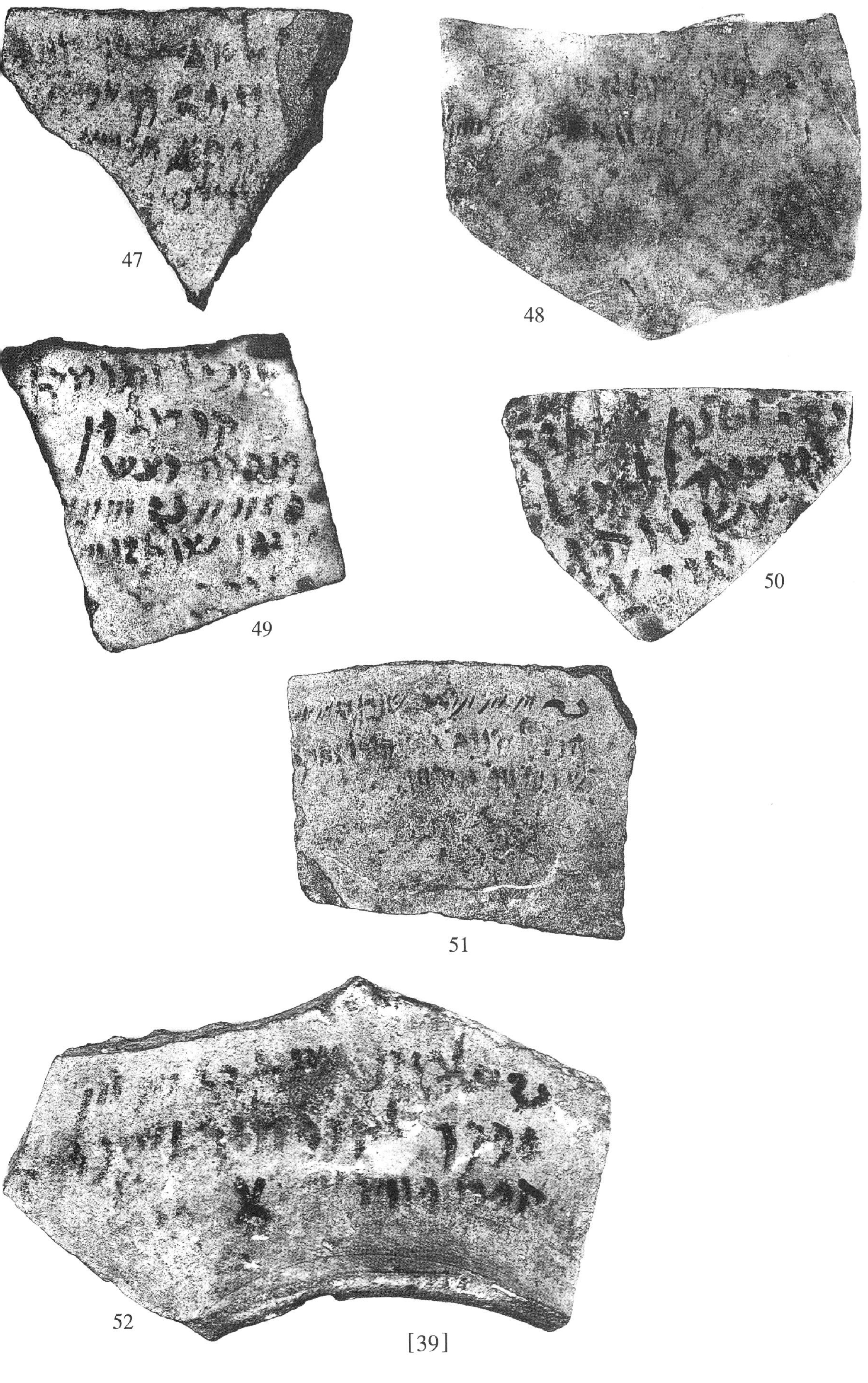

47 48 49 50 51 52

53	[On the Xth of S]ivan, year 46.	[ב X לס]יון שנת 46
	. . . to Qauskahel,	. . .] [לקוסכהל
	[fine flour: X *seah*], $1\frac{1}{2}$ *qab*, flour:	[נשיף ס X] ק 1 פ קמח
	[Y *seah*, Z *qab*] and a half.	[ס Y ק Z] פ

54	On the 3rd of Ab, year [+] 6.	ב 3 לאב שנת [+] 6
	La^{c}adel to . . .	לעדאל ל[. . .]
	in (the) pit . . .	במנקרה [. . .]
	. . . Sha^{c}adel	] [שעדאל
	(sign)	

55	On the 20th of Tebeth, year 2.	ב 20 לטבת שנת 2
	^{c}Abd$^{\supset}$ada of the Sons of	עבדאדה לבני
	^{c}Alba^{c}al, wheat: 5 *seah*,	עלבעל ח ס 5
	$3\frac{1}{2}$ *qab* . . .	ק 3 פ . . .

56	On the 25th of Tammuz, year 3.	ב 25 לתמוז שנת 3
	^{c}Abd$^{\supset}$ada son of Wahbi gave(?)	אתגנס עבדאדה בר והבי
	wheat: 24 *seah*, 2 *qab* to the hand of	ח ס 24 ק 2 על יד
	Ḥanael: 2 *sheqel* . . .	חנאל ש 2 ל 1

57	Nuhayru to Ba^{c}al^{c}id,	נהירו לבעלעיד
	five jars.	חביה חמש
	On the 29th of Ab,	ב 29 לאב
	year 4. ^{c}Abdmelek	שנת 4 עבדמלך
	b	ב

58	On the 7th of Elul, year 6.	ב 7 לאלול שנת 6
	^{c}Abd$^{\supset}$ada to Ḥanael,	עבדאדה לחנאל
	barley: 12 *seah* [. . .].	ש ס 12[ ]
	The owner of the storehouse (?) . . .	בעל מסכת[ ]
	barley: 4 *seah*, $4\frac{1}{2}$ *qab*.	ש ס 4 ק 4 פ

---

53 Between 21.6 and 19.7.359 BC
The reconstruction נשיף ס X is based on texts of other ostraca dealing with fine flour together with ordinary flour (קמח).

56 For אתגנס see Introduction, #21.

57 For חביה see Introduction, #16.

53

54

55

56

57

58

59	ʿAbdʾada to [. . .]lu . . . 6 *seah*, 3 *qab*.	עבדאדה ל[...]לו [ ] ס̄ 6 ק 3
60	On the 11th of Ab, year 1. . . . son of . . . . . . wheat: 2 *seah* (and) a *qab*.	ב 11 לאב שנת 1 [...] בר [...] [...] ח ס 2 קב
61	On the 1st of Tammuz, year 1, from Nutay[nu] son of Yehokal, wheat: 1 *kor*, 9 *seah*, 1 *qab*.	ב 1 לתמוז שנת 1 מן נתי[נו] בר יה̊וכל ח כ 1 ס 9 ק̄ 1
62	On the 8th of Marheshvan, year 2. ʿUbaydu of the Sons of Guru, barley: one *kor*, twelve *seah*, four *qab*.	ב 8 למרחשון שנת 2 עבידו לבני גורו ש̄ערן כר חד סאן עשר ותרתין קבן ארבעה
63	On the 11th of Kislev, year 2. Ḥabutu of the Sons of Guru, barley: eighteen *seah*, one *qab*.	ב 11 לכסלו שנת 2 חבותו לבני גורו שערן סאן עשר ותמ̊[נ]ה קב חד
64	[On the X of Mar]heshvan, ʿUbaydu [of the Sons of G]uru, wheat: seven *kor*.	[ב ... למ]רחשון עבידו [לבני ג]ורו חנטן כרן שבעה

62–64 (as well as No. 97) were written by the same person, who preferred to write the goods, measurements and numbers in full words instead of using the generally accepted abbreviated forms. Also in Nos. 150 and 152, which were presumably written by another hand, there are full words (cf. also Nos. 75 and 93). All these texts, which were written in relatively formal script and spelling, tend not to use abbreviations.

59

60

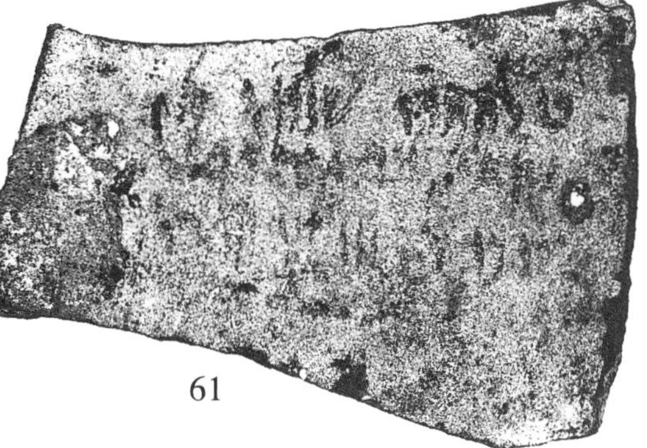
61

62

63

64

65	On the 6th of Iyyar, Mashru (or Mashku) of the Sons of Guru, wheat: three *seah*. Yatua^c (sign)	ב 6 לאיר משר/כו לבני גורו̄ ח̄ סאן תלת יתו̄ע ע
66	On the 28th of Tebe[th], crushed wheat: X *qab*. Gazri	ב 28 לטב[ת] דקיר ק[...] גזרי
67	^{c}Ubaydu of the Sons of Gir 20 *grgr*; 1 beam.	עבידו לבני גיר גרגרן 20 שרי 1
68	On the 22nd of Ab, yea[r X]. Zebadba^{c}ali to ^{c}Abd[...] of the Sons of Guru, wheat: 3 *seah*.	ב 22 לאב שנ[ת] זבדבעלי לעבד[ ] לבני גורו ח ס 3
69	^{c}Aliel of the Sons of Gur, 1 labourer.	עליאל לבני גור פעל 1
70	On the 22nd of Sivan, year 2 (?). Shartu(?), barley: 2 *seah*.	ב 22 לסיון שנת 2 (?) שר̄תו ש ס 2

65 66 67 68 69 70

71	On the 8th of Tammuz, year 2 [+]. Sha^cadi, wheat: 11 *seah*. Zebadel	ב 8 לתמוז שנת 2 [+] שעדי ח ס 11 זבדאל
72	On the 2nd of Marheshvan, year [3+]. Qausram of the Sons of ^cAlba^cal, from the grain of the purchase, wheat: 19 *seah*, . . . (a sign) ^cAlallahi	ב 2 למרחשון שנת 3 [+] קוסרם מן בני עלבעל מן עבור זבינת[א] ח ס 19 [ ] + עללהי
73	^cAnaniba^cal of the Sons of ^cAlba^cal, wheat: 2 *seah*.	ענניבעל לבני עלבעל ח ס 2
74	Zaydu son of Qanuy from [the Sons] of ^cAlba^cal, ...	זידו בר קנוי מן [בני] עלבעל [ ] . . .
75	On the 4th of Iyyar, Zabdi son of ^cAlba^cal brought in barley: thirteen *seah*.	ב 4 לאיר הנעל זבדי בר עלבעל שערן סאן עשרה ותלתה
76	Yaddua^c of the House of ^cAlba^cal, 15 *grgr*.	ידוע לבית עלבעל גרגרן 15

---

72 מן עבור זבינתא can be read also in Beer-sheba Ostracon No. 6.
עללהי is the Arabic personal name עְלאלהי; see also בני עללה in No. 118.

75 זבדי is written above the line; it was added later. This means that the person was called בר עלבעל.
סאן עשרה ותלתה. Here there is a mistake in genders. Since סאה is feminine, it should have been סאן עשר ותלת
In other ostraca the genders were used properly. See above, Nos. 62–64.

72

71

73

74

75

76

77	Qausmalak of the Sons of ^{c}Alba^{c}al, 6 sacks (of straw).	קוסמלך לבני עלבעל פחלצן 6
78	On the 24th of Ab, the Sons of Yehokal, Qausludan Qausludan . . .	ב 24 לאב בני יהוכל קוסלדן קוסלדן . . .
79	On the 2nd of Kislev, year 3. Samuk, wheat: 1 *seah*, . . .	ב 2 לכסלו שנת 3 סמוך ח[נ]טן ס 1 . . .
80	On the 6th of Kislev, year 3. Na^{c}um, fine flour: 1 *qab*; flour: $2^{1}/2$ *qab*.	ב 6 לכסלו שנת 3 נעום נשף ק 1 קמח ק 2 פ
81	On [the Xth of] Sivan, year 3. Qausluneṣar of the Sons of Yokal, to the storehouse of (the) pit, barley: 6 *kor*, 10 *seah*.	ב [X ל]סיון שנת 3 קוסלנצר לבני יוכל למסכנת מנקרה ש כרן 6 ס 10
82	On the 20th of Ab, year 4. Vanay, from the grain of the storehouse, wheat: 11 *seah*.	ב 20 לאב שנת 4 וני מן עבור מסכנתא ח ס 11

81 It seems that the date in line 1 was added after lines 2–4 were written.

82 For the name וני see Yadin and Naveh 1989:61–62 and note 9, and וניה in Ezra 10:36.

77
78
79
80
81
82

83	On the 20th of Ab, *Rwy* of the Sons of Ba^{c}alrim, oil: 1 *seah*, 1 *qab*.	ב 20 לאדר רוי לבני בעלרים משח ס 1 ק 1
84	The Sons of Ba^{c}alrim, on the 20th of Ab, ^{c}Abdqaus.	בני בעלרים ב 20 לאב עבדקוס
85	Qausram of the Sons of Ba^{c}alrim, barley: 28 *seah*, . . . to . . . to Zamru.	קוסרם לבני בעלרים ש ס 28 [. . .] ל[. . .] לזמרו
86	Zubayd of the Sons of Ba^{c}arim, one beam. On the 28th of Ab.	זביד לבני בערים שרי חדה ב 28 לאב
87	On the 2nd of Shebat, Zebad$^{\supset}$ada son of Naqru of the House of Ba^{c}alrim, 2 labourers.	ב 2 לשבט זבדאדה בר נקרו לבית בעלרים פעלן 2
88	Ḥazira, crushed wheat: 1 *seah*, 3½ *qab*. On the 19th of Tammuz, year 6.	חזירא דקר ס 1 ק 3 פ ב 19 לתמוז שנת 6

---

86 בערים is בעלרים.

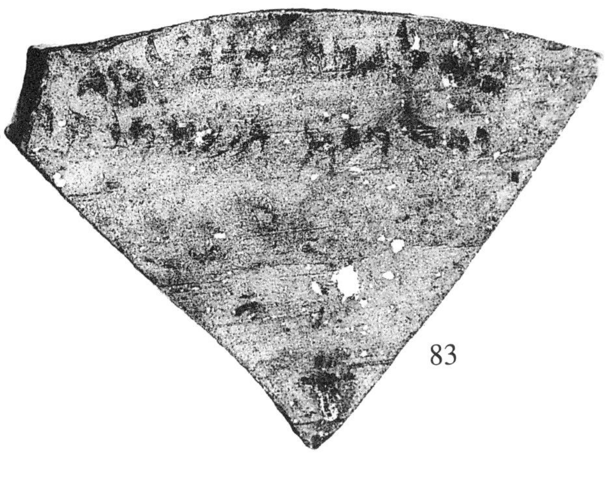
83

84

85

86

87

88

89	Qausmalak,	קוסמלך
	crushed wheat: $3^{1}/_{2}$ *seah*.	דקר ס 3 פ
	On the 9th of Ab,	ב 9 לאב
	year 6.	שנת 6
90	On the 5th of Sivan, year 7.	ב 5 לסיון שנת 7
	Na^{c}um brought from Ramta, to the hand of	היתי נעום מן רמתא̄ על יד
	Agra, to the storehouse, wheat: 16 *seah*.	אגרא למ[סכנ]תא ח ס 16
91	On the 9th of Elul, year 7.	ב 9 לאלול שנת 7
	^{c}Abdshamash, wheat: 28 *kor* (?).	עבדשמש ח כ̄ 28
92	On the 11th of Ab, year 7.	ב 11 לאב שנת 7
	^{c}Alqaus of the Sons of Qoṣi, to the hand of	עלקוס לבני קוצי ליד
	Ḥazael, from the loan, wheat: 10 *seah*,	חזאל מן זפתא ח ס 10
	to the storehouse, wheat: 20 *seah*.	למסכנתא ח ס 20
93	^{c}Alqaus of the Sons of Qoṣi,	עלקוס לבני קוצי
	flour: three *seah*, four	קמח סאן תלת קבן
	qab.	ארבעה
	On the . . . of . . .	ב. . . ל. . .
94	Yitaḥ of the Sons of Qoṣi,	יתאח לבני קצי
	3 jars. On the 8th	חביה 3 ב 8
	of Elul.	לאלול

---

90 רמתא is either a geographic name or a topographic indication; see Introduction, #26.
אגרא was the name of the father of Rabbi Yehudah and the father-in-law of Rabbi Abba (B. T. Ḥullin 104b, 134a; Niddah 53a). אגרה was inscribed on two ossuaries from Jerusalem; see Milik 1958:96, Nos. 32–33.

89

90

91

92

93

94

95 The Sons of Qosi,
3 labourers.

בני קוסי
פעלן 3

96 On the 2nd of Adar, year 3 of Philip the king.
^{c}Abdosiri of the Sons of Yehokal,
wine: 16 *seah*, to the hand of
Ḥaggai and Zebadallahi.
Yatua^{c}

ב 2 לאדר שנת 3 פלפס מלכא
עבדאוסירי לבני יהוכל
חמר ס 16 על יד
חגי וזבדאלהי
יתוע

97 On the 12th of Kislev, year 7
of Philip the king. Zebad$^{\supset}$ada son of
Qaus^{c}adar, from the horse-ranch of Garpa,
barley: 3 *kor* to the hand of Ḥalfan.

ב 12 לכסלו שנת 7
פלפס מלכא זבדאדה בר
קוסעדר מן רכשת גרפא
ש כרן 3 על יד חלפן

98 On the 10th o Kislev, year 2 {.}
^{c}Alqaus son of Ḥuri brought in,
as the tribute of Philip, to the hand of
^{c}Abdisi, oil:
3 *seah*.

ב 10 לכסלו שנת 2 {.}
הנע̊ל עלקוס בר חורי
אשכר פלפוס ליד
עבדאסי משח
ס 3

99 On the 1st of Tammuz, Qaus^{c}adar,
wheat: 1 *kor*, 12(?) *seah*, 1 *qab*.

ב 1 לתמוז קוסעדר
ח כר 1 ס 12(?) ק 1

100 On the 4th of Tammuz,
Qaus^{c}adar son of ^{c}Alqaus,
from ^{c}Arbat Ḥanzaru,
wheat: 10 *kor*.
Netina wrote (it).
(a sign)

ב 4 לתמוז
קוסעדר בר עלקוס
מן ערבת חנזרו
ח כ 10
נתינא כתב

---

96 14.3.320 BC

97 11.12.317 BC
The name גרפא occurs in the papyrus from Ketef Yeriḥo (Eshel and Misgav 1988:169) and in Nabataean as גרפו. It seems likely that גלפא (No. 150) is a variation of the same name.

98 The sign following the number 2 is unclear.
אשכר meaning 'tax, tribute' occurs in Ps. 72:10 and in the fifth-century inscriptions on the green chert objects from Persepolis (Introduction, # 22). In Ezek. 27:15 it seems to mean 'finished products, staples or materials, to be delivered' (cf. *iškaru* A, 3, *CAD* I/J 246–48). A sixth-century BC Aramaic inscription on a jar from Kadesh Barnea reads אשכר טבין[..] (Cohen 1983:12). In Neo-Assyrian texts *iškaru* means a kind of tribute or tax (see *iškaru* A, 4, *ibid.*, 248; Postgate 1974:94–110). Although in these texts we find the combinations '*iškaru* of the king' and '*iškaru* of the king's mother', such a combination as '*iškaru* + PN (a king's name)' does not occur. One may, therefore, consider that אשכר פלפוס may be associated with a tax-collector rather than with the king.

95

96

97

98

99

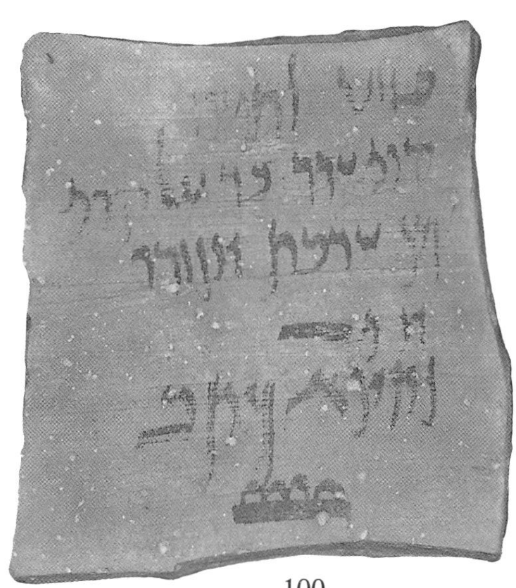

100

101 On the 25th of Sivan, year 10.
Namru to Zabdi, barley: 20 *seah*.

ב 25 לסיון שנת 10
נמרו לזֿבֿדֿי ש ס 20

102 On the 16th of Adar, year 13.
^{c}Abd$^{\supset}$ada, wheat meal:
8 *seah*.

ב 16 לאדר שנת 1̄3̄
עבדאדה קמח חנטן
ס 8

103 On the 22nd of Shebat, year 14.
Ḥanael, wheat meal: . . .
. . .

ב 22 לשבט שנת 14
חנאל קמח חנטן [ ]
. . .

104 On the 30th of Sivan, year 16.
Bdn to Zubaydu, flour:
3 *qab*. (sign + signature)

ב 30 לסיון שנת 1̄6
בדן(?) לזבידו קמ̄ח
ק̄ 3 . . .

105 On the 14th of Elul, year 16.
Sha^{c}adi son of . . . to Ḥalfan,
wheat: 4 *seah*.

ב 14 לאלול שנת 16
שעדי בר [. . .] לחלפן
ח ס 4

106 On the 14th of Tebeth, year 17.
Qoṣ(?) of the House of Yehokal,
wheat: 16 *seah*, $1^{1}/_{4}$ *qab*.

ב 14 לטבת שנת 17
ק̄ו̄ץ̄ לבית יהוכל
ח ס 16 ק 1 ר 1

101
102
103
105
104
106

107	On the 2nd of Tammuz, year 19. Shu[c]aydu of the Sons of *Rwy*, wheat: 5 *seah*, 4 *qab*. 20 *b*.	ב 2 לתמוז שנת 19 שעידו לבני ר̄וי ח ס 5 ק 4 ב 20
108	On the 18th of Tammuz, year 5. Nahru gave(?) to (the) pit, barley: 2 *kor* to the hand of *Prḥd* and in Malḥat, (on) that day, Qausmalak, barley: 1 *seah*.	ב 18 לתמוז שנת 5 אתגנ[ס] נה̄רו למנקרה ש כ 2 על יד פרחד ובמלחת יומא הו קוסמלך ש ס 1
109	On the 14th of Ab, year 1. [c]Alqaus son of [c]Edri, wheat: 6 *seah*, 4 [*qab*]. Zebadel	ב 14 לאב שנת 1 עלקוס בר עדרי ח ס 6 [ק] 4 זבדאל
110	On the 20th of Marheshvan, year X [c]A[l]qaus, barley: 6 *seah*, 5 *qab*.	ב 20 למרח̄שון שנת [. . .] ע[ל]קוס ש ס 6 ק 5
111	. . . . On the 20th of Shebat, year 5 of Alexander the king.	. . . . ב 20 לשבט שנת 5 אלכסנדר מלכ[א]
112	To Ḥalfan, fodder(?): . . . On the 5th of Kislev, y[ear X] of Alexander the king.	לחלפן שחת̄[ ] ב 5 לכסלו ש[נת X] אלכסנדר מלכא

---

107 ב does not seem to stand for a measure-unit since, according to our document, it should be less than $^{1}/_{20}$ a *qab*. Such a fraction of a *qab* is too small when grain is concerned.

108 מלחת is presumably a toponym.

111 22.2.311 BC

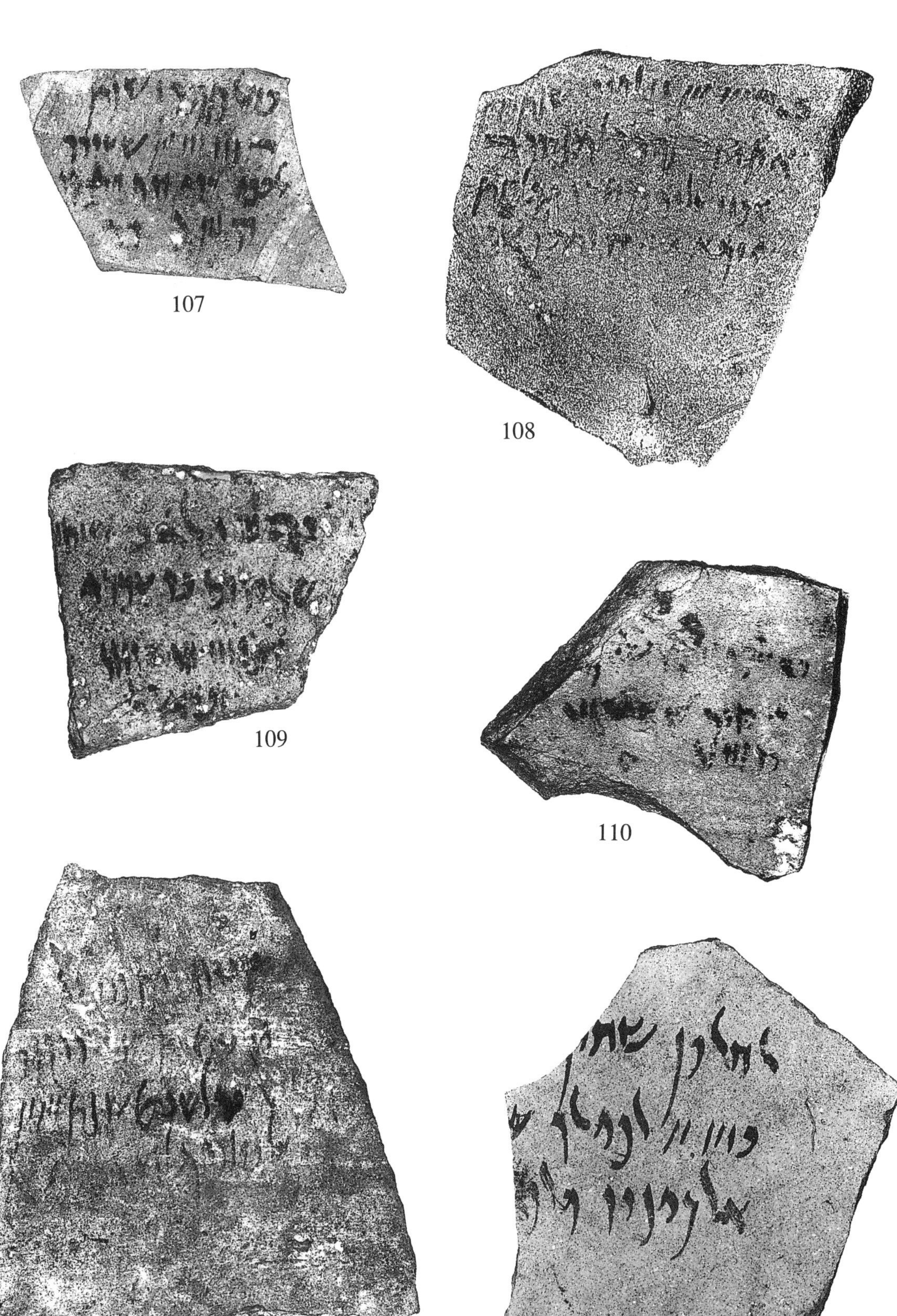

107

108

109

110

111

112

113	Qawwehlael	קוהלאל
	son of ᶜAlqaus,	ר עלקוס
	oil: 2 *seah.*	משח ס 2
114	On the 12th of Tebeth,	12 לטבת
	Qoṣi brought 1 *grgr.*	יתי קצי גרגר 1
115	[Ḥa]nael son of Naqru,	ח]נאל בר נקרו
	oil: 2 *seah,*	משח ס 2
	$3^3/4$ *qab.*	ק 3 ר 3
116	Pelaṭel to Zubaydu,	פלטאל לזבידו
	. . . under the authority of	] על יד
	. . .	. .
117	On the 14th of Tebeth,	14 לטבת
	Shuᶜaydu, barley groats: 3 *seah.*	שעידו רוש ס 3
118	A cow for sacrifice(?),	תורתא לעלוה חד
	. . . for atonement(?) / to the village(?). . .	. . לכפרא זיק אף
	. . .	. .
	4 labourers: 3 Sons of	פעלין בני
	[Gur?]u, 1 (of the) Sons of ᶜAlallah.	גור?]ו 3 בני עללה 1

---

118 Reading and interpretation of lines 1–2 is uncertain.
בני עללה see עללהי, No. 72.

113

114

115

116

117

118

119	Netina, 3 jars from the Sons of . . .	נתינ̅א חביה 3 מן בני [. . .]ינא
120	On the 27th, Ba^{c}alḥanan to Qausram, wheat: 1 *kor*.	ב 27 בעלחנן לקוסרם ח כ 1
121	Zaydu son of Na^{c}um, oil: $4^{1}/_{2}$ *qab*; wheat: 1 *seah*, 3 <*qab*>. On the 18th of Elul.	זידו בר נעום משח ק 4 פ ח ס 1 <ק> 3 ב 18 לאלול
122	. . . Qausluneṣar owes 20 *ma^{c}ah* . . . were striped from the fringes . . . [. . . +]3 [*seah*], 4 *qab*.	] על קוסלנצר מ 20] חטיבו מן ציציתא] ר̅פיד̅ +]3 ק 4
123	Ḥalfan and Sham^{c}u, flour: 13 *seah*, 3 *qab*.	חלפן ושמ̅עו קמח ס 13 ק 3
124	. . . to Da^{c}^{ɔ}el [from (the) p]it, oil: [X *seah*], $5^{1}/_{2}$ *qab*.	]וי לדעאל מן מנ]קרה משח ס X] ק 5 פ̅

---

121 For the omission of ק see Naveh 1992a:49-50.

122 קוסלנצר (Qaus indeed guarded [me]); ל (=*lu*) is an affirmative particle; compare with personal names like אדנלרם on an eighth-century BC brick inscription from Hamath (*KAI*, No. 203). Otherwise, the reading and interpretation of the text is difficult.
Line 2 presumably deals with some garments.

119

121

120

122

123

124

	Translation	Text
125	Qausdekar, barley: 1 *qab*.	קוסדכר ש ק 1
126	ᶜAbdᵓada, flour(?): 3 *seah*, 4 *qab*. On the day (?) . . .	עבדאד̅ה ק̅מ̅ח̅ ס 3 ק 4 ב̅י̅ו̅ם̅ [ ]
127	. . . . . . On the 20th Tamm[uz] crushed wheat: 2[+] *seah*.	[ ] [.]שוי ב 20 תמ[וז] דקקירא̅ ס 2 [+]
128	On the 18th of . . . gave (?) . . .	ב 18 לא[ ] אתגנס̅ [ ]
129	Naᶜum to Ḥanae[l] 1 load (of wood).	נעום לחנא[ל] מו̅בל 1
130	On the 10th of Sivan . . . from ᶜArbat [. . .] . . .	ב 10 לסיון [ ] מן ערבת א[ ] . . .

---

127 Is דקקירא a corruption of דקיר, or some plural form?

129 For מובל designating a load of wood see Introduction, #14.

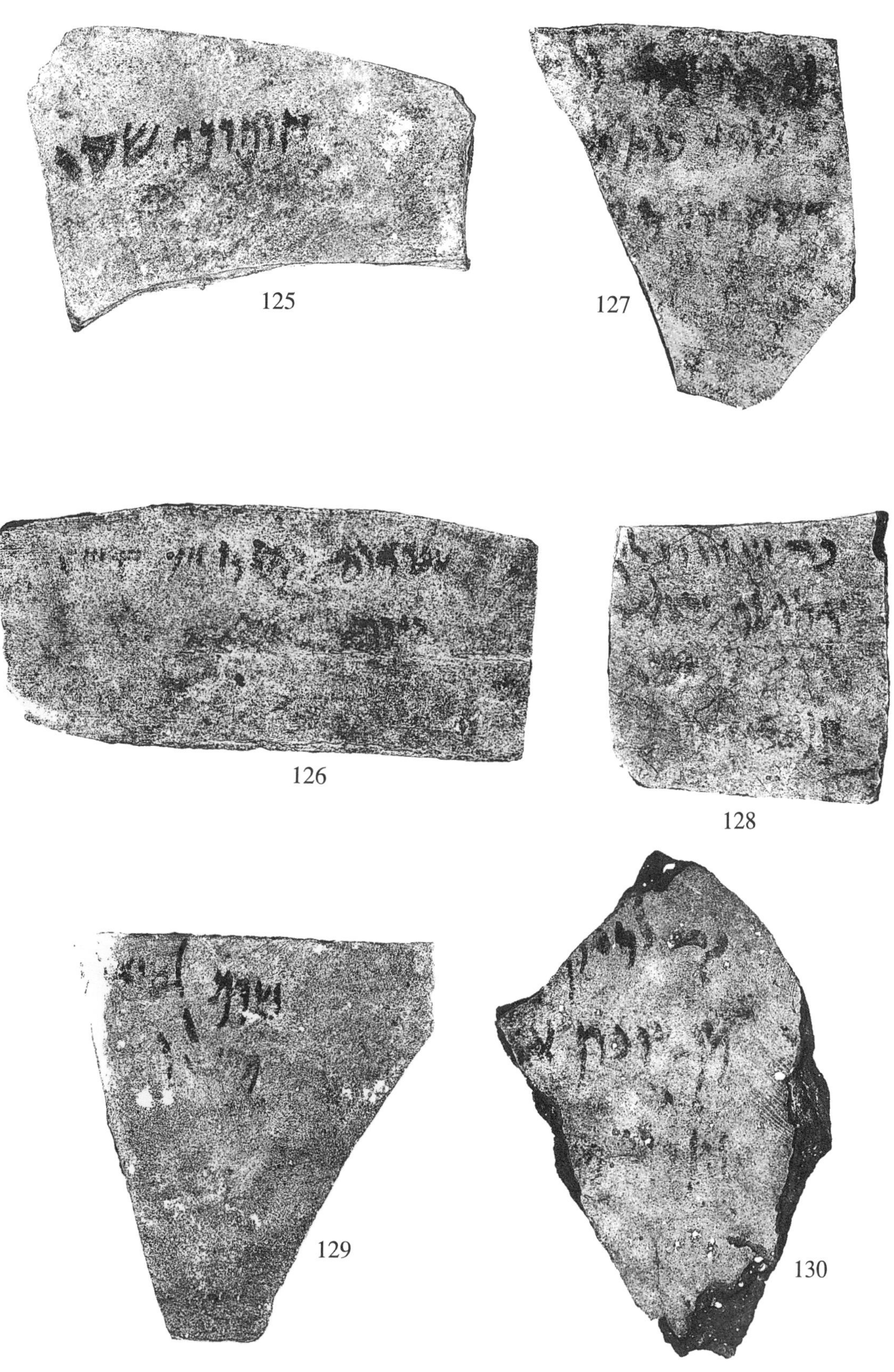

125 127

126 128

129 130

131	(From the) pit to . . . of the House of . . .	מקרה ל[ ] לבית קו[ ]
132	[. . .]zebad and Qausyehab to . . . 2 [ba]skets (of straw).	[ ]זבד וקוסיהב ל[ ] [מ]שתלן 2
133	Qausram . . . . . . On . . . of . . .	קוסרם [ ] פסי[ ] ב. . . ל. . .
134	Qausyehab, crushed wheat: 6 *seah*, 1 *qab*.	קוסיהב דקר ס 6 ק 1
135	They divided the ladders(?): hundred and 44.	חלקו סלמיא מא ו 44
136	Naqru to El^{c}ali, straw: 7 baskets.	נקרו לאלעלי תבן משתלן 7

---

135 See above, commentary on No. 15 for the mixed way of writing the number 144.

131

132

133

134

135

136

137	Ḥuri to Ḥaggai, wheat: 1 *qab*.	חורי לחגי̅ ח ק 1
138	Flour(?) for oil: 1 *seah*, 4 *qab*.	ק̅מ̅ח̅ במשח ס 1 ק 4
139	Shallum to Qauskahel, from the grain of . . . barley: 7 *seah*, 2 *qab*.	שלום לקוסכהל מן עבור [. . .] ש ס 7 ק 2
140	To *Bnk*, silver: 2 *ma*ᶜ*ah*. *Bwsm* owes to *Yw*[ ] 2 quarters.	לבנך כסף מ 2 על {ב} בוסם ר 2 ליו[ ]
141	Qauskahel, 10 *sheqel*, $1^1/2$ *ma*ᶜ*ah* Shartu(?), 30 *sheqel*.	קוסכהל ש 10 מ 1 פ שר̅תו ש 30
142	One *sheqel* will belong to the robbers(?)	ש חד לבזין יהוי

---

140 The reading is very conjectural.

141 For the equation:

שקל,	*sheqel*	(tetradrachma)	1		
רבע,	quarter	(drachma)	4	1	
מעה,	*ma*ᶜ*ah*	(obolos)	24	6	1

cf. Milik 1961:90–91.

142 The reading and interpretation are uncertain.

137

138

139

141

142

140

143	On the 1st of Elul, Qanuy, barley: 4 *kor*. . . .	ב 1 לאלול קנוי ש כ 4 מעונין/מעון 2
144	On the 20th . . . flour: X *seah*, . . . and a *qab* to our gate(?).	ב 10[ ] קמח ס [ ] וקב[ ] לתרען
145	. . . . . . 4 [*seah*], 3 *qab*. . . . . . . crushed wheat: 2 *seah*, 1 *qab*. (sign + signature)	[ ]ן ט[ ] [ ]4 ק 3[ ] [ ]דקיר ס 2 ק 1 . . .
146	On the 1st of Nisan, Zaydel	ב 1 לנסן זידאל . . . . . .
147	On the 10th ^{c}Uwaydu	ב 10 עוידו
148	. . . to ^{c}Obadyahu	[ ]לעבדיהו

---

143 The reading מעונין / מעון is very problematic. An alternative reading 2 מעין (2 *ma^{c}ah*) cannot be associated with 4 *kor* of barley.

144 Does לתרען (to our gate) mean 'to our price'? See Eph^{c}al and Naveh 1993.

148 לעבדיהו. See above, commentary on No. 16.

143

144

145

146

147

148

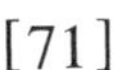

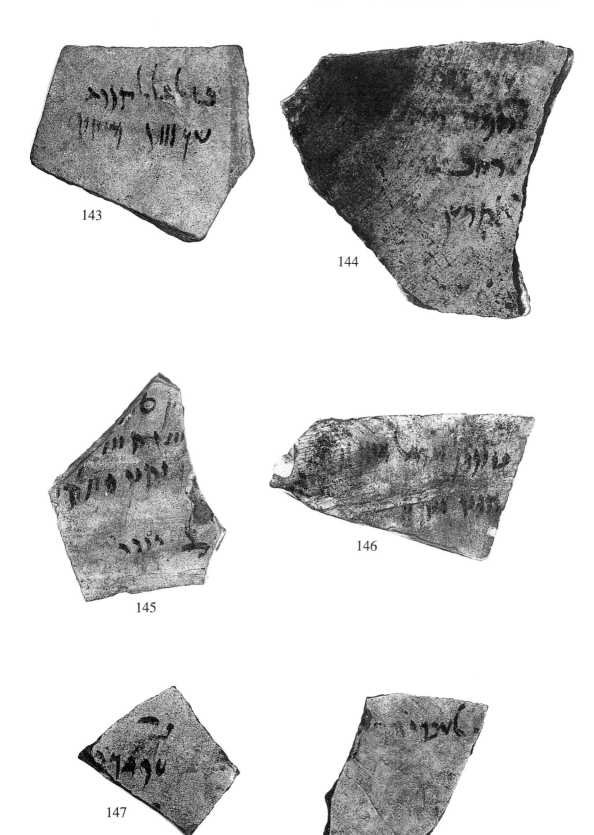

149	On the 9th . . .	ב 9[ ]
	^{c}Abdba^{c}al and . . .	עבדבעל ו[ ]
150	On the 1st of Nisan, the Sons of Rammarana	ב 1 לניסן בני רממרן
	to the owners of (the) pit, wine:	לבעלי מנקרה חמר
	twenty *seah*; pine (seed): 2 *qab*,	סאן עשרן ער ק 2
	under the authority of Galpa and De^{c}imarana.	על יד גלפא ודעימרן
151	. . . to (the) pit . . .	[ ]י למנקרה [ ]
	1 goat hi[de].	[מ]שך ענז 1
152	On the 26th of Tammuz, Qausgad	ב 26 לתמוז הנעל
	brought in wheat: two *seah*	קוסגד חנטן סאן תרתין
	and a *qab* and a half.	וקב חד ופלג
153	[On] the 20th of Adar(?) Qaushanan	[ב] 20 לאדר היתי קוסחנן
	[son of Q]uaskahel brought barley: 20 *seah*,	[בר ק]וסכהל ש ס 20
	to the hand of Qausmalak.	עליד קוסמלך
154	[. . . +]6	[+]6
	. . . Barley: 1 *kor*, 16 *seah*	[ ] ש כ 1 ס 16
	. . . Qausram; and a half	[ ] קוסרם ופלג
	. . . baskets (of straw).	[ ] משתלן

---

150 רממרן and דעימרן are names (the latter is a feminine name) compounded with the theophoric element מרן (Marna, Marnas). See עבדמראן (^{c}Abdmarana) on the ostracon from Raphia (Naveh 1985:118–19).
גלפא is presumably a variant of גרפא in No. 97.
For the unabbreviated writing in Nos. 150 and 152 see above, Nos. 62–64.

154 The relation between lines 3 and 4 is not clear.

149

150

151

152

153

154

155 Ḥalfan, 2
grgr; 1 basket (of straw).

חלפן גרגרן
2 משתל 1

156 ^{c}Aydu to Maliku,
27 *grgr*.

עידו למלכו
גרגרן 27

157 On the 29th of Shebat.
Zabda, X *grgr*.

ב 29 לשבט
זבדא גרגרן [ ]

158 Ṣuran(?) son of Qaus^{c}ani, 3 loads (of wood).

צורן בר קוסעני מובלן 3

159 Nutaynu to Marṣe^{c}at,
barley: 1 *qab*.

נתינו למרצעת
ש ק 1

160 On the 17th of . . .
^{c}Ani, wheat: 5 *seah*.
Zebadel

ב 17 לא[. .]
עני ח ס 5
זבדאל

---

158 צורן is not clear.

155

156

157

158

159

160

161	On the 13th of Tammuz, ye[ar X].	ב 13 לתמוז שנ]ת [
	^{c}Ani, wheat: 6[+] *seah*,	עני ח ס 6]+ [
	$5^{1}/_{2}$ *qab*.	ק 5 פ
162	Zubaydu son of ^{c}Idaḥ	היתי זבידו
	brought from . . .	בר עידאח מן [. .]ון
	Ba^{c}al[ ]	בעל[ ]
	son of ^{c}Abdba^{c}ali, 2 sacks (of straw).	בר עבדבעלי̄ פחל<צ>ן 2
163	On the 8th of Nisan, Qaus^{c}ani of the Sons of	ב 8 לניסן קוסעני לבני
	Ba^{c}alrim (?), 53 *grgr*.	בעלרם (?) גרגרן 53
164	On the 13th of Kislev, Qaus^{c}ani son of	ב 13 לכסלו קוסעני בר
	. . .	. . .
	oil: . . . to the hand of	משח . . . על יד
	. . .	. . .
165	. . . son of . . .	[ ]ו בר לה[ ]
166	. . .	. . .
	. . .	. . .
	wheat: 2 *kor*, 1 *seah*, 5 *qab*.	ח̄ כ 2 ס 1 ק 5

161 This document is the verso of 160. The two texts are independent of each other.

161

163

162

164

165

166

167	On the 27th of Elul, to the hand of Shimri, . . ., Shaᶜadi and ᶜAlqaus, wood: 3 loads.	27 לאלול על יד שמרי א[. .]ל שעדי ועלקוס עקן ובלן 3
168	wheat: 23(?) *seah*, tribute . . .	ז ס 23(?) שכרא . . .
169	Refuse of cast straw: . . . bas[ket]. Refuse . . . a basket.	פי תבן שדי ש]תל [פי[ ] שתל
170	Refuse of cast straw: a basket.	פה תבן שדי שתל
171	Refuse of cast straw: a basket.	פי תבן די משתל
172	(Belonging to) Marṣeᶜat	מרצעת

168 אשכרא see above, commentary on No. 98.

169 For עפי תבן שדי see Introduction, # 13b.

172 למרצעת is written below the handle of the jar.

167

169

168

171

170

172

173	Qaushạnan	קוסחנן
174	. . . wheat: 5 *qab*	*recte* וזא [. . . .] ח ק 5
	. . . $4\frac{1}{2}$ *qab*	[. . .] ק 4 פ
	Ba^{c}alḥan and Ḥiel 4 *seah*, $3\frac{3}{4}$ *qab*	בעלחן וחיאל ס 4 ק 3 ר 3
	^{c}Otni 6 *seah*, 3 *qab*	עתני ס 6 ק 3
	Ḥazira $4\frac{1}{2}$ *qab*	חזירא ק 4 פ
	Qausyeta^{c} 1 *seah*, $1\frac{3}{4}$ *qab*	קוסיתע ס 1 ק 1 ר 3
	. . . from . . .	*verso* [. . .] מן [. . .]
	to Qausludan 5 *qab*	לקוסלדן ק 5
	Ḥanina 5 *qab*	חנינא ק 5
	Ṭubyau $4\frac{1}{2}$ *qab*	טביו ק 4 פ
	that is what Qausyeta^{c} will give to Ṭubyau, $2\frac{1}{2}$ *qab*	זי ינתן קוסיתע לטביו ק 2 פ
	and Ḥazira will give him 3 *qab*	וינתן לה חזירא ק 3

175	Qauslunesạr	^{c}Aydan	עידן	קוסלנצר
	Marse^{c}at	. . .	. . .	מרצעת
	^{c}Abdel	. . .	. . .	עבדאל
	Qausyinqom	Ba^{c}alsamak	בעלסמך	קוסינקם
	Nahru	^{c}Abdallahi	עבדלהי	הרו
	Wahabel	. . .	. . .	הבאל
	^{c}Alqaus			לקוס
	Qausner			קוסנר

176	Qausnetan 2	קוסנתן 2
	. . . 1	1 . .
	Netanba^{c}al 2	תנבעל 2
177	Qausnetan and Lael,	קוסנתן ולאל
	wheat: $2\frac{1}{2}$ *seah* to	ס 2 פ לות
	. . .	. .

---

173 קוסחנן was written perpendicularly on a jar.

174 טביו may be the Hebrew name Ṭubyau (see below, the fifth-century BC name list, No. 201:4); but it migh also be an Arabic name ending with -u.

173

175

174

176

177

No.	Translation		Text	
178	^{c}Ubaydu	El^{c}id	עבידו	אלעיד
	Ḥanina	. . .	חנינא	. . .
	Qausḥanan	Gahmu	קוסחנן	גהמו
	. . .	^{c}Aynab(?)	ע[. . .]	ע̄ינ̄ב̄
	Ḥalfat		חלפת	
	Zubaydu		זבידו	
179	Ramqaus, wheat: $4^{3}/_{4}$ *qab*,		רמקוס ח ק 4 ר 3	
	^{c}Abd$^{\supset}$ada, wheat: 1 *seah* . . .		עבדאדה ח ס 1 [. . .]	
	La^{c}adel, wheat: $2^{1}/_{4}$ *qab*.		לעדאל ח ק 2 ר 1	
	. . .		. . .	
180	Silver . . . the Sons of		כס̄ף [. . .] בני	
	Qausmalak, 2 *sheqel*;		קוסמלך ש 2	
	. . . 4 *sheqel*;		. . . ש 4	
	. . .		. . .	
	La^{c}adel, X *sheqel*.		לעדאל ש . . .	
181	[. . .]melek		[. . .]מלך	
	Zebadmelek		זבדמלך	
	Sons of . . .		בני . . .	
	Ba^{c}alrim		בעלרם	
	. . .		. . .	
	Wahbi		והבי	
	. . .		. . .	
182	Ḥabutu		חבותו	
	^{c}Ubaydu		עבידו	
	Ḥanan		חנן	
	Ḥuzayru		חזירו	
	^{c}Abdosiri		עבדאוסרי	
	Ḥabutu		חבותו	
	Zaydel		זידאל	
183	Qausyinqo[m]		קוסינק[ם]	
	Ṭubyau to [ ]		טביו ל[ ]	

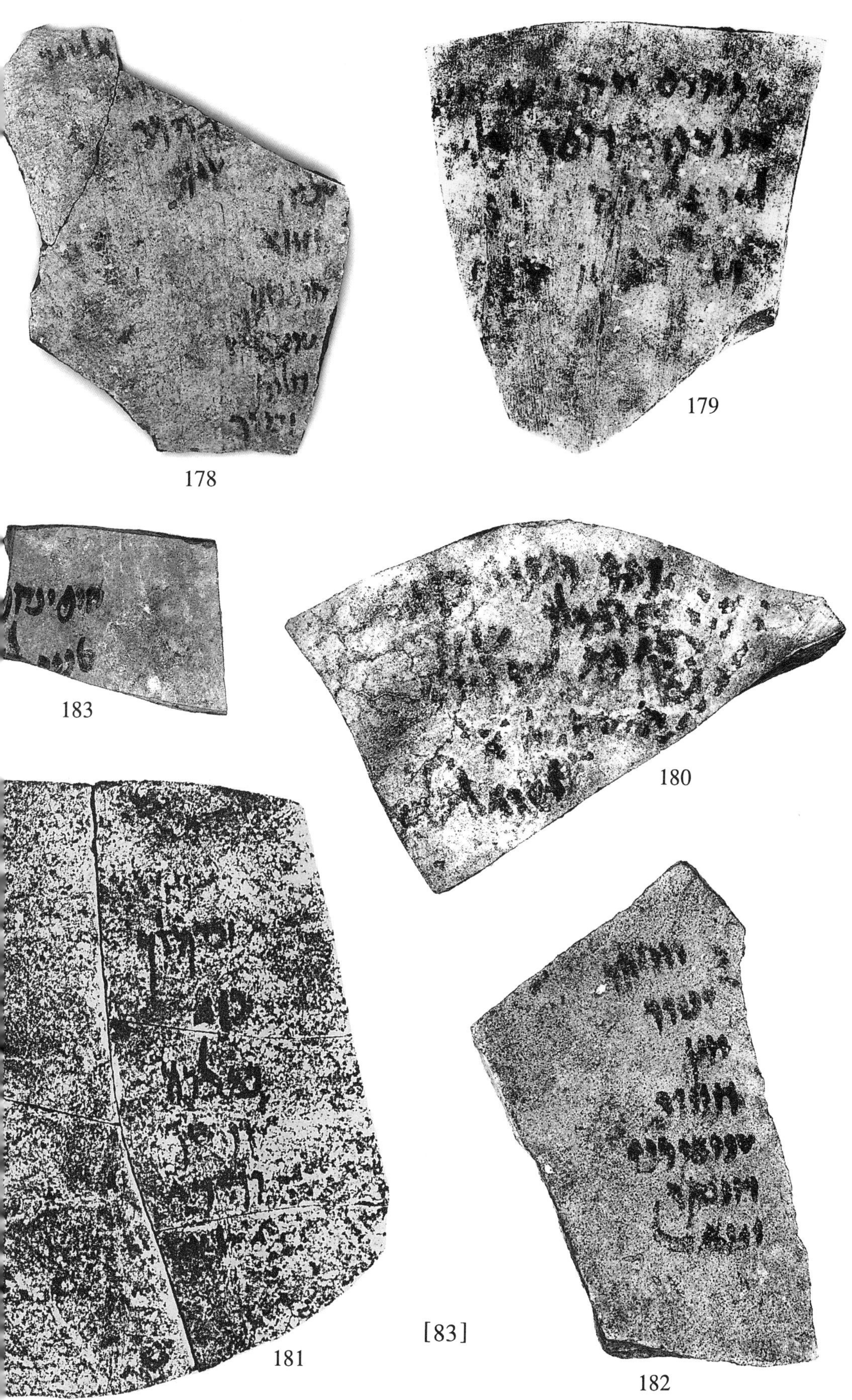

178

179

183

180

181

182

184	Shamu[.], 2 quarters (of a *sheqel*)	‏זמו[.] ר 2
	Aḥimeh, 2 quarters	‏חמה ר 2
	Shamashdan, 2 quarters	‏ממשדן ר 2
	Maṭran, 2 quarters	‏טרן ר 2
	[. . .]ʿadar, 2 quarters	‏. .]עדר ר 2
	(*on the right*:) ʿAbdʾada, 2 quarters	‏בדאדה ר 2
	(*on the left*:) ʿUwaydu . . .	‏וידו [. . .]
185	. . .	. .
	(in addition) to it . . .	‏לוהי [ ]
	the garden of Qaus[. . .]	‏נת קוס[ ]
	the olives of *kph*	‏תי כפה
	(in addition) to it . . .	‏לוה . . .
186	The olives of Samuk: 3 *kor*	‏תי סמוך כ 3
	the olives of Qausram: 1 *kor*	‏תי קוסרם כ 1
	lighting (olives): 1 *kor*, 10 *seah*	‏אור כ 1 ס 10
	thus . . .: 1 *kor*	‏ות ג[ ] כ 1
	divided (?) to 10 . . .	‏רוס על 10 א[. . .]
187	The olives . . .	‏תיא . . .
	the tax-collector, 3 *kor*, 15 *seah*	‏באא כרן 3 ס 15
	the portion of the first, 13 *seah*	‏רסת קדמיה ס 13
	the olives of the last , X *kor*	‏תיא זי אחרי כ [ ]
	1 *kor* of lighting olives, . . .	‏1 זיתי מאור כ[ ]
188	The vineyard of Ḥuri: 26 *seah*	‏רם חורי ס 26
	ḥlṣ of the *rbyns*: 12 *seah*	‏לץ רביניא ס 12
	rpyd of the *msgrs*: 16 *seah*	‏פיד מסגריא ס 16
	kpy of ʿAzgad: 16 *seah*	‏פי עזגד ס 16
	The vineyard of *brʾ*: 14 *seah*	‏רם ברא ס 14
	The vineyard of ʿOtni: 26 *seah*	‏רם עתני ס 26
	(*on the side*:) altogether: 3 *kor*, [X *seah*]	‏ל כרן 3 [סאן X]

---

185 The West Semitic word גנת also occurs in the Greek documents from the archive of Babatha from the Ba Kokhba period (see Lewis 1989, Nos. 21:9, 10; 22:10, 11). It occurs there in the consruct state (γαννα PN = 'the garden of PN'), as in our document. The same Greek documents contain the word *κήπο* (garden, orchard). Can כפה, כפי in our Aramaic documents be a word borrowed from Greek, having th same meaning?

188 The amount of seeds needed for sowing the total area of the units listed in this document is 110 *seah*, i.e 3 *kor*, 20 *seah*.

184

185

186

187

188

	Translation	Text
189	Plots of land: the orchard of ᶜAliel: a land for sowing 2 *seah*; *ṣrṣr*ᵓ [X] *seah*;	זלקן נצב עליאל זרע ס 2 צ̄רצ̄רא ס[ ]
	the vineyard of Binu: 8 *seah*; the vineyard of ᶜAliyu: 4 *seah*, 4[+] *qab*	רם בינו ס 8 כרם עליו ס 4 ק 4 [+]
	In the vineyards of Sismay: 11 *seah*, 3 *qab*: from a quarter of the lot of . . .	כרמי ססמי ס 11 ק 3 מן רבע אשל ש[ ]
	the white (field): a quarter of the *kph* (?) of Ḥazael: 6 *seah*, $4^1/2$ *qab* . . .	זורא רבע כפת חזהאל ס 6 ק 4 פ [ ]
190	5 *seah* . . .	5 [ ]
	. . .	. .
	the olives (or: olive groves) of *rpyd*ᵓ: 13 *seah*	יתי רפידא ס 13
	the field of ᶜAmi: 1 *kor*, 5 *seah*	זור עמי כ 1 ס 5
	the field of Baᶜali, from Ḥuri (?)	זור בעלי מן ח̄ו̄ר̄י̄
	Baᶜalguru: a *kor*	עלגורו כר
191	. . . the measurements of Qausyetaᶜ: $1^1/2$ *ašlu*	. . .]יא משחת [.] קוסיתע אשל 1 פ
	. . . 9 *ašlu* . . .	. . .] אשלן 9 [ ]
	. . . $1^1/4$ *ašlu*, 15 cubits in width	. . .] אשל 1 ר 1 אמן 15 ל̄פ̄ת̄י̄
	. . . marsh: X *ašlu* . . .	. . .] רקק אשלן [. . .]
	. . .	. .
192	The lot(?) of . . .	אשלא זי [ ]
	and the vineyard of . . .	כרם קו[ ]
	rpyd of Qaus[. . .]	פיד קוס[ ]
	The half of . . .	לג שק[ ]
	The lot (?) of . . .	אשל גל[ ]
	ḥlṣ of . . .	זלץ [ ]
	. . .	. .
193	The plot of *Rwy* . . .	זלק ר̄וי י[ ]
	The *kph* of *Rmk* . . .	כ̄פת רמך מ[ ]
	portion by po[rtion . . .]	זלקה בח[לקה]
	. . .	. .

---

189 The original meaning of *ašlu* in Akkadian is 'rope', 'cord', and secondarily 'measuring line' — a rop[e] used for measuring. On חבל (usually 'rope') as a measuring line cf. 2 Sam. 8:2; and on חבל מדה, 'measurin[g] cord' cf. Amos 7:17 and Zach. 2:5. Another meaning of חבל in Hebrew is 'lot', 'portion', cf. Ps. 78:55[;] Deut. 32:9; Josh. 17:5. The expressions [...] אשלא זי = 'the *ašlu* of ...' (Nos. 192:1, 195:1) and אשל פל'= 'th[e] *ašlu* of PN' (Nos. 192:5, 194:2) cannot be interpreted as referring to a linear measure (as in No. 191[.]) Presumably, אשל(א) in our text means 'lot', 'portion', like חבל in Hebrew.

189

190

192

191

193

No.	Translation	Text
194	*rpyd* of the white (soil?) and the lot(?) of Qausram	ר̅פ̅י̅ד̅ חורתא ואשל קוס̅ר̅ם̅
195	The lot(?) of . . . 6 [+] *seah* . . . 4 *qab*.	אשל זי [ ] ס 6 [+] ק 4
196	If my lord pleases, let them free the daughter of Ḥaggai.	הן על מראי טב ישבקו ברת חגי
197	Qausmalak, you . . . that I . . . no . . .	קוסמלך אנת [ ] זי אנה ח[ ] לא
198	and a servant in your hand . . . to Qausmalak . . . If	ועלים בידך א[ ] לקוסמלך [ ] הן ת[ ] . . .

194 From the feminine word חורתא, alongside the masculine רפיד, one may infer that the reference is to ארעא חורתא (the white [soil]).

196–198 Written by the same person, these documents seem to be partial drafts of a letter.

194 195 196 197

198

Translation		Text
199 1. The buyer who promised to give me the money,	1	זבונא זי הקים למנתן לי כספא
2. did not give [it]. He said thus to me: "why do you	2	לא יהב כן אמר לי למה מסחר
3. beg (or: trade) in my place? there is no money". And the debt	3	אנת באתרי כסף לא איתי וחבא
4. that . . . the money that has been left on his account,	4	זי מה(. .)ף כסף זי שאר עלויה
5. is 1 *ma^{c}ah*. It has been said, as we saw, you did not	5	מ 1 מתאמר כזי חזין {.} לא
6. pay the man's / collector's respect. Now, if he comes	6	הקבלת לגבר/יא כען הן אתה
7. there, give (pl.) him one of the slave-girls,	7	תמה הבו לה חדה מן עלימתא
8. and the rest will remain in debt.	8	ושאריתא בחב יהוי

---

199 This document is written on both sides of the same sherd, each containing four lines. It is difficult to decide whether the text is a draft or an informal letter (without address and greeting formula). The reading and the somewhat free translation above are partly tentative.

Line 1. We translated הקים 'he promised'. נשבע ('he swore') in Gen. 24:7 is translated in the Jewish Targums by קיים in *pa^{cc}el*, whereas in the Peshitta it is אקים, in *aph^{c}el*.

Line 4. עלויה is a parallel form of עלוהי. The phrase כסף זי שאר עלויה means 'the money that he still owes'.

Line 5. כזי חזין = 'as we saw' or 'as they are seen'. In the legal documents from Wadi Murabba^{c}at and Naḥal Ḥever, the expression כזי חזי means 'as proper' (Yadin 1962:249), the Hebrew cognate of which is כראוי.

Line 6. הקבל may perhaps be the *haph^{c}el* of קבל meaning 'to give'; compare with הקחת, a *haph^{c}el* form of לקח, in Naḥal Ḥever (Lewis 1989, No. 18:68). However, it may also have a similar meaning to the Hebrew expression הקבל פנים.

גבר/יא: either גברא or גביא; the latter is preferable.

Line 8. ושאריתא בחב יהוי should be ושאריתא בחב תהוי.

199

	Translation	Text
200	These are who . . .	אלה זי] [
	that *Rws* is his name . . .	י רוס שמה כ] [
	Ḥashabyau son of Laṣra . . .	י חשביו בר לצרא] [
	Ḥananyau his brother	חנניו אחוה[י]
	[Yeh]okal, ᶜAzzur his son . . .	יה]וכל עזור בר[ה [
	. . . son of Mika[. . .]	] בר מכ[[
	. . . son of Gilgal . . .	] בר גלגל [
201	. . . money . . .	]מה כסף] [
	Qausner son of Gilgal, Ḥashabyau son of Laṣra,	קוסנר בר גלגל חשביו בר לצרא
	Yehokal, ᶜAzzur his son 1, ShemaᶜJayah son of Tibnah,	יהוכל עזור ברה 1 שמעיה בר תבנה
	YehoᶜJaz son of Ḥigger-Ur, Ṭubyau son of Shemaᶜaya[h].	יהועז בר חגר אור טביו בר שמעי[ה]
	These men(?) will give the provision of the servants of . . .	נשאן אלה ינתנן פתפה זי עלימי] [
	1 named Peṭis, named Aḥḥapi, ᵓsršwt . . . named *Šmw*	פטיס שמה 1 אחחפי שמה אסרשו[ת] שמו שמה

200 and **201** were written by the same hand in the first half of the 5th century BC. These are fragmentary name lists, listing partly the same persons, who should supply the provisions of some servants. Whereas the former have mostly Hebrew names (Qausner is an Edomite name), the four servants listed in No. 201:6–7 have Egyptian names; אסרשות is a feminine name (see Cowley 1923, No. 34:3 and Kornfeld 1978:78) לצרא is presumably a variant of נצרא.

The spelling of the Yahwistic element -יהו as the first component of personal names (יהועז and יהוכל in No. 201:4–5), and יו- as the second component (חשביו and טביו in No. 200:3 and 201:4, respectively), accords with the spelling of this element in Jewish names known from the epigraphic sources. Thus, for example the fifth-century BC Neo-Babylonian inscriptions (esp. the Bīt Murašû documents, dated 455–403 BC) have *Ia-(a-)ḫu-(u)* at the beginning of names and *-ia-(a-)ma* at the end (cf. Zadok 1979:7–11; the ending יו- in Nos. 200–201 may remove some of Zadok's hesitations about the Babylonian rendering of this component). For the יו- ending, see the contemporary names אוריו and חלקיו (Avigad 1957:146–153; 1965:230–232, respectively). The spelling שמעיה in No. 201:3 (and perhaps also in line 4) is an exception. The meaning of נשאן in No. 201, line 5, is not clear. Instead of ... אלה ינתנן פתפה זי עלימי, it should be ינתנן פתפהון זי עלימי, or פתפא זי עלימי.

201 Ḥigger, meaning 'lame', may be a nickname for Ur.

200

201

GLOSSARY

Line numbers printed in italics represent uncertain readings

אב month Ab 10:1, 37:3, 54:1, 57:3, 60:1, 68:1, 78:1, 82:1, 84:1, 86:3, 89:3, 92:1, 109:1, 160:*1*

אדר month Adar 42:2, 83:1, 96:1, 102:1, 153:*1*. אדר אחרי Second Adar 11:1, 28:3,

אחרי last, later 11:1, 28:3, 187:4. אחריא 4:3, 5:3; see also אדר

איר month Iyyar 1:1, 65:1, 75:1

איתי (there) is 199:3

אלול month Elul 6:1, 7:1, 8:1, 20:1, 58:1, 91:1, 94:3, 105:1, 121:3, 143:1, 167:1

אמה cubit. אמן 191:3;

אמר to say 199:2. מתאמר 199:5

אמר lamb. אמרן 46:3

אנה I 197:2

אנת you 197:1, 199:3

ארבעה four 62:4, 93:3

אשכר tax, tribute 98:4. אשכרא 168:2

אשל *ašlu* (a linear measure) 191:1, 3. אשלן 191:2,4

אשל lot(?) 189:3, 192:5, 194:2, 195:1. אשלא 192:1.

אתי to come. אתה 199:6. היתי to bring 1:2, 13:2, 27:1, 31:1, 33:1, 35:1, 90:2, 114:2, 153:1, 162:1

אתר place. באתרי in my place, after me 199:3

ב־ on (in date formula) 1:1, 2:1, 3:1, 4:1, 5:1, 6:1, 7:1, 8:1, 9:1, 10:1, 11:1, 12:2, 13:1, 14:1, 15:1, 16:1, 17:1, 22:2, 24:1,3, 28:2, 31:1, 35:1, 37:3, 38:3, 41:4, 42:4, 43:1, 44:3, 46:1, 48:1, 49:4, 50:1, 51:1, 52:1, 54:1, 55:1, 56:1, 57:3, 58:1, 60:1, 61:1, 62:1, 63:1, 65:1, 66:1, 68:1, 71:1, 72:1, 75:1, 78:1, 79:1, 80:1, 81:1, 82:1, 83:1, 84:1, 86:3, 87:1, 88:3, 89:3, 90:1, 91:1, 92:1, 93:4, 94:2, 96:1, 97:1, 98:1, 99:1, 100:1, 101:1, 102:1, 103:1, 104:1, 105:1, 106:1, 107:1, 108:1, 109:1, 110:1, 111:1, 112:2, 114:1, 117:1, 120:1, 121:1, 126:*1*, 127:2, 128:1, 130:1, 143:1, 144:*1*, 146:1, 147:1, 149:1, 150:1, 152:1, 157:1 160:1, 161:1, 163:1, 164:1, 167:1. ב־ in 2:3, 54:3, 108:3, 189:3, 198:1, 199:3,8. ב־ for 138:2. ב־ other meanings 107:4, 133:3, 193:3

בז robber. בזין (?) 142:1

ביו house (of) 76:1, 87:*2*, 106:2, 131:2

בע owner 58:*4*; בעלי 150:2

בר son (of) 1:3, 3:2, 4:2, 11:2, 25:2, 40:2, 47:1, 49:2, 56:2, 61:2, 75:1, 87:2, 97:2, 98:2, 100:2, 105:2, 109:2, 113:2, 115:1, 121:1, 158:1, 162:1,4, 164:1; בני sons of 41:2, 42:1, 55:2, 62:2, 63:1, 65:2, 67:1, 68:3, 69:1, 72:1, 73:1, 77:1, 78:1, 81:2, 83:1, 84:1, 85:1, 86:1, 92:2, 93:1, 94:1, 95:1, 107:3, 118:4,5, 119:2, 150:1, 163:1, 180:1

ברה daughter. ברת 196:3

גבי collector. גביא (or גברא) 199:6. גבאא 187:2

גבר man. גברא (or גביא) 199:6

גנה garden. גנת 185:3

גנס to store(?). אתגנס 56:2, 108:2, 128:2

גרגר meaning unknown 114:2. גרגרן 22:1, 67:2, 76:2, 155:1, 156:2, 157:2, 163:2

דבר to drive, take 46:1

דכר ram 46:3

דמין price, payment. דמי 16:3

דקיר crushed (barley/wheat) 66:2, 145:3. דקר 89:2, 88:1, 134:1. דקקירא 127:*3*

הו he, it. See יום

הוי to be. יהוי 142:1, 199:8

הן if 196:1, 198:3, 199:6

ו־ and 31:2, 42:2, 44:2, 46:2, 62:3, 63:2, 75:3, 96:4, 108:3, 123:1, 132:1, 135:2, 144:3, 149:2, 150:4, 152:3, 154:3, 167:2, 174r.3, 174v.6, 192:2, 199:3,8

זבון buyer. זבונא 199:1

זבינה purchase, merchandise. זבינתא *72:3*

זי of, which 1:4, 2:2, 42:2, 174v.5, 187:4, 192:1, 194:1, 195:1, 197:2, 199:1,4. See also כזי

זית olive, olive grove. זיתיא 187:*1*, 4. זיתי 185:4, 186:1.2, 187:5, 190:3

זפה loan. זפתא 47:3, 92:3

זרע seed 189:1

ח see חנטן

חב debt 199:8. חבא 199:3

חביה jar(s) 57:2, 94:2, 119:1

חד one 62:3, 63:3, 118:*1*, 142:1, 152:3. חדה 86:2, 199:7

חור white. חורא 189:4. חורתא 194:1

חיוה animal. חיון 46:3

חזי to see. חזין 199:5

חטב to stripe, embroider. חטיבו 122:2

חלץ meaning unknown. 188:2, 192:6

חלק to divide. חלקו 135:1

חלק plot 193:1. חלקן 189:1

חלקה portion 193:3

חמר wine 96:3, 150:2. חמרא 16:3

חמשה five. חמש 57:2

חנטן wheat 64:2, 79:2, 102:2, 103:2, 152:2. חנטיא 35:2. ח 2:*3*, 8:2, 12:1, 13:4, 15:3, 29:1, 31:2, 34:3, 35:3, 44:*2*, 47:2, 48:*2*, 55:3, 56:3, 60:3, 61:3, 65:*3*, 68:3, 71:3, 72:4, 73:*2*, 82:3, 90:3, 91:2, 92:3,4, 100:4, 105:3, 106:3, 107:3, 109:3, 118:6, 120:3, 121:2, 160:2, 161:2, 166:*3*, 168:2, 174r.1, 177:2, 179:1-3

טב good 196:2

טבת month Tebeth 46:1, 50:1, 55:1, 66:*1*, 106:1, 114:1, 117:1

טור field 190:4,5

טחון grind 1:3. טחונא 4:3, 5:2

יד hand. ידך 198:1. ליד to the hand of 2:2, 92:2, 98:4. על יד to the hand of, under the authority of 34:2, 37:2, 56:3, 90:2, 96:3, 97:4, 108:3, 116:2, 150:4, 153:3, 164:3, 167:1

יהב to give 16:2, 199:2. הבו 199:7

יום day 126:*2*. יומא הו on that day 108:4

כ see כר

כות thus 186:4

כזי at the time that, when 199:5

כל all, altogether 188:7

כן so, thus 199:2

כסלו month Kislev 16:1, 41:5, 63:1, 79:1, 80:1, 97:1, 98:1, 112:2, 164:1

כסף silver, money 140:1, 180:*1*, 199:3,4. כספא 199:1

כען now 199:6

כפה garden 185:3. כפת 189;4, 193:*2*. כפי 188:4

כפר village. כפרא (?) 118:2

כפרא atonement (?) 118:2

כר *kor* 13:3, 62:3, 99:2, 190:6. כרן 33:2, 34:3,4, 35:3, 64:2, 81:4, 97:4, 187;2, 188:7. כ 2:*3*, 9:3, 13:4, 29:*1*, 61:3, 92:*2*, 100:4, 108:3, 120:3, 143:2, 154:2, 166:3, 186:2-4, 187:4-*6*, 190:4

כרם vineyard 188:1,5,6, 189:2, 192:2. כרמי 189:3

כתב to write 100:5

ל־ of (in date formula) 1:1, 2:1, 3:1, 4:1, 5:1, 6:1, 7:1, 8:1, 9:1, 10:1, 11:1, 12:2, 13:1, 14:1, 15:1, 16:1, 17:1, 19:2, 22:2, 28:2, 31:1, 33:2, 35:1, 37:3, 38:3, 41:5, 42:4, 43:1, 44:3, 46:1, 48:1, 49:5, 50:1, 51:1, 52:1, 54:1, 55:1, 56:1, 57:3, 58:1, 60:1, 61:1 62:1, 63:1, 66:1, 68:1, 70:1, 71:1, 72:1, 75:1, 78:1, 79:1, 80:1, 82:1, 83:1, 84:1, 86:3, 87:1, 88:3, 89:3, 90:1, 91:1, 92:1, 93:4, 96:1, 97:1, 98:1,4, 99:1:1, 100:1, 101:1, 102:1, 103:1, 104:1, 105:1, 106:1, 107:1, 108:5, 109:1, 110:1, 111:1, 112:2, 114:1, 117:1, 121:3, 129:1, 131:1, 133:3, 143:1:1, 146:1, 150:1, 152:1, 153:*1*, 157:1, 160:1, 161:1, 163:1, 164:1, 167:1. ל־ to 1:2, 3:2, 4:2, 5:2, 9:2, 14:2, 16:2, 18:1, 19:1, 20:1, 21:1, 22:1, 23:1, 25:1, 34:2, 37:1, 38:1, 39:1, 41:1, 43:1, 45:1, 49:1, 50:2, 52:2, 58:2, 59:1, 62:2, 63:1, 65:2, 68:2, 81:3, 85:3,4, 90:3, 92:3, 98:4, 101:2, 104:2, 105:2, 108:2, 112:1, 116:1, 120:2, 124:1, 128:1, 129:1, 136:1, 137:1, 139:1, 140:1,2, 142:1, 144:4, 148:1, 150:2, 151:1, 156:1, 159:1, 172:1, 174v.2, 198:2. ל־ of (the sons/house of) 67:1, 68:1, 69:1:1, 73:1, 76:1, 77:1, 81:2, 83:1, 85:1, 86:1, 87:1, 92:2, 93:1, 94:1, 96:2, 106:2, 107:3, 131:2, 163:1. ל־ for 56:4, 118:1,2. לי 199:1,2,6. לה 174v.6, 199:7

לא no, not 197:2, 199:2,3,5

ליד see יד

לות to, near 177:2

למה why? 199:2

מ (for מעה) *ma*^{c}*ah*, obolos 16:3, 122:1, 140:1 141:1, 199:5

מאה hundred. מא (?) 135:2

מאור lighting 186:3, 187:5

מובל load 25:2, 129:2. מובלן 158:1, 167:3

מטא to arrive. המטא to deliver, bring 26:1

מלך king. מלכא 13:2, 96:1, 97:2, 111:*4*, 112:3

מן from 1:3, 4:2, 5:2, 15:*2*, 26:2, 34:1, 38:1, 41:1 42:1, 46:2, 47:2, 49:2, 61:1, 72:2, 82:2, 90: 92:3, 97:3, 100:3, 119:2, 122:2, 130:2, 139: 162:2, 174v.1, 189:3, 190:5, 199:7

מנקרה pit 2:3, 9:2, 34:1, 38:2, 49:3, 54:3, 81: 108:2, 124:*2*, 150:2, 151:1. מקרה 15:*2*, 131

מסגר generally prison, but in the context of סגריא in 188:3 unclear

מסכ storehouse. מסכנתא 25:*2*, 82:2, 90:*3*, 92:4. מסכנת 47:*3*, 81:3. מסכת 58:4
מסנ nail, peg. מסמרן 28:1
מקו see מנקרה
מר lord. מראי 196:1
מרחש month Marheshvan 22:2, 44:3, 62:1, 64:*1*, 72:1, 110:*1*,
מש oil 11:3, 17:*3*, 32:1, 83:2, 98:5, 113:3, 115:2, 121:2, 124:2, 138:2, 164:3
משח measurement. משחת 191:1
מש hide. [מ]שך 151:2
משו basket (for straw) 37:2, 155:2, 169:*2*,4 170:2, 171:2. משתלן 24:2, 36:1, 45:2, 132:*2*, 136:2, 154:4. משתלין 24:*4*

ני month Nisan 42:2, 49:5, 150:1, 163:1. נסן 146:1
נ plant, orchard 189:1
נש fine flour 3:3, 5:3, 6:2, 7:2, 26:2, 30:1, 48:*2*, 52:2. נשף 80:2
נו to give 1:4. ינתן 174v.5,6. למנתן 199:1

see סאה
סא *seah.* סאן 15:3, 62:3, 63:2, 65:3, 75:2, 93:2, 150:3, 152:2. ס 1:5, 2:*3*, 3:3, 4:4, 5:3, 6:2,3, 7:3, 8:2, 9:3, 12:1, 13:3, 14:3, 26:3, 29:1, 31:2, 32:1, 33:2, 34:3, 35:*3*, 42:3, 44:*2*, 47:2, 48:2, 49:4, 50:3, 51:3, 52:2,3, 55:*3*, 56:3, 58:3, 59:*2*, 60:3, 61:3, 68:2, 70:2, 71:3, 72:4, 73:*2*, 79:2, 81:4, 82:3, 83:2, 85:2, 88:2, 89:2, 90:3, 92:3, 96:3, 98:5, 99:2, 101:2, 102:3, 105:3, 106:3, 107:3, 108:4, 109:3, 110:2, 115:2, 117:*2*, 121:2, 123:2, 124:3, 134:2, 138:2, 139:3, 144:2, 149:3, 153:2, 154:2, 160:2, 161:2, 166:3, 168:2, 174r.3,4,6, 177:*2*, 79:2, 186:3, 187:2,3, 188:1-6, 189:1-4, 190:1,3,4, 195:2
סו to trade, beg, go around. מסחר 199:2
סי month Sivan 3:1, 9:1, 12:2, 33:2, 38:*3*, 42:4, 43:*1*, 47:1, 52:1, 53:*1*, 70:1, 81:1, 90:1, 91:1, 101:1, 104:1, 130:1
סל ladder. סלמיא 135:1

עב grain 47:2, 72:3, 82:2, 139:2
ע on 140:2, 185:*5*, 186:*5*, 196:1. עלוהי 185:2. עלויה 199:4. על פל׳ PN owes 122:1, 140:2. על יד see יד
עלו sacrifice (?) 118:1
עלי slave 198:1. עלימתא 199:7
על to enter. הנעל to bring in 34:1, 51:2, 75:1, 98:*2*, 152:1
ע goat 151:2

עפי refuse, stench 169:1,3, 171:1. עפה 170:1
עק wood. עקן 25:2, 167:2
ער pine, pine seed 150:3
ערבה wilderness(?). ערבת 100:3, 130:2
עשרה ten 75:2. עשר 62:3, 63:2
עשרן twenty 150:3

פ see פלג
פחלץ sack (of straw) 19:2. פוחלץ 38:*2*. פחלצן 18:2, 23:2, 77:2. פחל‹צ›ן 162:4
פלג half 10:2, 32:2, 152:3, 154:3, 192:4. פ 30:1, 37:2, 53:3,4, 55:4, 58:5, 80:3, 88:2, 89:2, 121:2, 124:*3*, 141:1, 161:3, 174r.2,5, 174v.4,5, 177:2, 189:4, 191:1
פעל labourer 69:2. פעלן 87:*3*, 95:2. פעלין 118:*4*
פרס to divide. פרסת 187:3. פרוס 186:5
פתי width. לפתי 191:*3*

ציצי fringe. ציציתא 122:2
צרצר cricket. צרצרא (name of an orchard?) 189:*1*

ק see קב
קב *qab* 10:*2*, 15:3, 32:2, 60:3, 144:3, 152:3. קבן 62:*4*, 63:*4*, 93:2 ק 1:5, 3:3, 4:4, 5:3, 6:3, 7:2,3, 9:3, 11:3, 12:1, 13:3,*4*, 30:1,2, 31:3, 32:2, 34:3, 41:3, 42:3, 48:2, 50:3, 51:*3*, 52:2,3, 53:3, 55:4, 56:3, 58:5, 59:2, 61:*3*, 66:2, 80:2,3, 83:2, 88:2, 99:2, 104:*3*, 106:3, 107:4, 110:3, 115:3, 121:2, 122:4, 123:3, 124:3, 125:1, 134:2, 138:2, 139:3, 145:2,3, 150:3, 159:2, 161:3, 166:3, 174r.1-6, 174v.2-4,5,6, 179:1,3, 189:2-4, 195:3
קבל to receive. הקבלת 199:6
קדם before, in front of. קדמיה 187:3. מן קדם from 46:2
קום to arise, stand. הקים to promise 199:1
קמח flour 3:3, 4:*3*, 5:4, 6:3, 7:3, 30:2, 44:1, 53:3, 80:3, 93:2, 102:2, 103:2, 104:*2*, 123:2, 126:*1*, 138:*1*, 144:2
קשת grove 39:1, 40:1

ר see רבע
ראש see רוש
רביניא ? 188:2
רבע a quarter 189:3,4. ר 191:3 (רבע אשל), 6:2, 11:3, 35:3, 106:3, 115:3, 140:2, 174r.3,6, 179:1,3 (רבע קב), 184:1–6 (רבע שקל)
רוש barley groats 117:2. ראש 1:4, 41:*3*, 42:*3*, 49:3, 50:*3*
רחל ewe 46:3
רכשה horse ranch. רכשת גרפא 97:3

רפיד ? 122:*3*, 188:*3*, 192:3, 194:*1*. רפידא 190:3
רקק marsh 191:4

ש see שערן
ש (for שקל) *sheqel* 141:1,2, 142:1, 180:2,3,5
שאר to remain 199:4
שארי rest, remainder. שאריתא 199:8
שבט month Shebat 15:1, 17:1, 87:1, 103:1, 111:3, 157:1
שבעה seven 64:2
שבק to leave, abandon, let free. ישבקו 196:2
שדי to throw, cast out 169:1, 170:1, 171:2
שחת fodder (?) 112:1
שנה year. שנת 1:1, 2:1, 3:1, 4:1, 5:1, 6:1, 7:1, 8:1, 9:*1*, 11:2, 12:2, 13:1, 14:1, 15:1, 17:2, 41:*5*, 43:*1*, 48:1, 49:5, 50:1, 51:2, 52:1, 53:1, 54:1, 55:1, 56:1, 57:4, 58:1, 60:1, 61:1, 62:1, 63:1, 68:*1*, 70:1, 71:1, 72:1, 79:1, 80:1, 81:1, 82:1, 88:4, 89:4, 90:1, 92:1, 96:1, 97:1, 98:1, 101:1, 102:1, 103:1, 104:1, 105:1, 106:1, 107:1, 108:1, 109:1, 110:1, 111:3, 112:*2*, 139:3, 161:1
שערן barley 34:4, 62:*2*, 63:2, 75:2. ש 9:3, 10:2, 13:3, 14:3, 29:*1*, 31:2, 33:2, 51:3, 56:4, 58:3,5, 70:2, 81:4, 85:2, 97:4, 101:2, 108:3,4, 110:2, 125:1, 143:2, 153:2, 154:*2*, 159:1
שרי beam 67:2, 86:2

ת (for תומנה) an eighth (*qab*) 11:3, 17:3
תבן straw 136:1, 169:1, 170:1, 171:1
תורה cow. תורתא (?) 118:1
תלתה three 75:3. תלת 65:3, 93:2
תמה there 199:7
תמוז month Tammuz 2:1, 4:1, 5:1, 13:1, 14:1, 35: 56:1, 61:1, 71:1, 88:3, 99:1, 100:5, 107:1, 108: 152:1, 161:1
תמניה eight. תמנה (fem.) 63:*2*
תרין two. תרי 15:3. תרתין 62:3, 152:2
תרע gate. תרען 144:4

Glossary of Nos. 200 and 201

אח brother. אחוה[י] 200:4
אלה these 200:1, 201:5
בר son (of) 200:3,6.7, 201:2,3,4. ברה 200:5, 201
זי relative/possessive pronoun 200:1,2,3, 201:5
כסף silver, money 201:1
נשאן men (?) 201:5
נתן to give. ינתנן 201:5
עלים slave. עלימי 201:5
פתף portion. פתפה 201:5
שם name. שמה 200:2, 201:6,7

INDICES OF NAMES

Personal Names
in Nos. 1–199

Toponyms

Personal Names in Nos. 200–201